Beyond Listening

Beyond Listening

Learning the Secret Language of Focus Groups

BONNIE GOEBERT

with
Herma M. Rosenthal

John Wiley & Sons, Inc.

Published by John Wiley & Sons, Inc., New York.
Published simultaneously in Canada.

This publication is designed to provide accurate and authoritative information in regard to the subject matter covered. It is sold with the understanding that the publisher is not engaged in rendering professional services. If professional advice or other expert assistance is required, the services of a competent professional person should be sought.

Designations used by companies to distinguish their products are often claimed as trademarks. In all instances where John Wiley & Sons, Inc. is aware of a claim, the product names appear in initial capital or all capital letters. Readers, however, should contact the appropriate companies for more complete information regarding trademarks and registration.

Library of Congress Cataloging-in-Publication Data:

Goebert, Bonnie
    Beyond listening: learning the secret language of focus groups / Bonnie Goebert with Herma M. Rosenthal.
      p. cm.
    Includes index.
    ISBN 0-471-39562-5 (cloth : alk. paper)
    1. Consumers' preferences. 2. Consumer behavior. 3. Focused group interviewing. I. Rosenthal, Herma M. II. Title.

HF5415.32.G64 2001
658.8'3–dc21

2001045637

Printed in the United States of America.

10 9 8 7 6 5 4 3 2 1

For my mom, Molly,
whose curiosity is unrelenting

PREFACE

You're watching TV and see a newscaster standing in a torrential downpour, reporting on a hurricane with gale force winds in the Carolinas. As he tries to hold his microphone steady so that the station logo faces the camera, he doesn't seem terribly safe himself. Behind him, humongous waves are crashing and thrashing to shore, and he tells you that all traffic is stopped, roads are impassable, and everyone is advised to stay home. As you stare at him being buffeted by winds and water, you're not focusing on the hurricane but wondering to yourself, "Hey, how did this guy get there and how is he going to get back to his hotel room?"

We talk to ourselves all the time. Most of these inner thoughts never surface. They reflect the same kind of internal dialogue we have when we stand at a supermarket shelf to select paper towels or stop to take a closer look at a magazine ad for a new cell-phone service or decide whether to use a credit card to pay for gas. Our running commentary is often so subliminal that we forget it's going on.

As a focus group moderator, I reach out to consumers in my groups and try to drag that kind of information out of them and into the foreground. What I do is a kind of marketing therapy that reveals how we as consumers feel about a product, a service, an ad, or a brand. Is the reporter-in-a-hurricane disconnect going on when we look at a commercial? What kind of silent conversation are we conducting that might shed light on why we're so discriminating about certain brands and can't remember the names of others or why a particular product has so embedded itself in our lives that we find even the slightest change threatening?

Having conducted market research for more than three decades, I've not only seen what's behind consumer perception, motivation, and behavior but also peered into the corporate psyche. The companies that tune in to the consumer frequency—who are willing to listen to simple as well as complex truths—understand how to crash through the clutter and adapt to changing customer attitudes and desires.

This is especially important today when a well-tuned brand is your company's best equity. To understand your own brand and how best to communicate its intangible values to your core customers, you must know how that consumer base feels about your brand and recognize its place in a wide competitive field. We all bond to brands today. We rely on them more than ever to deliver benefits that reflect our own values, respect our needs, and fulfill our desires. Careful listening to how consumers talk about their favorites and why they're loyal (or not) is the only way you'll truly understand this unique relationship and develop the necessary insights that will push your brand out in front for the long term.

My goal isn't to teach people how to conduct a focus group but to heighten awareness of the dialogue that takes place between consumers and the products and services they use, and the brands they favor. Many companies only vaguely understand who their customers are, how those customers really react to what marketers and advertisers pitch them, and what happens when they arrive at—or after they leave—the retail environment, in itself a term that has taken on new meanings. For the consumer today, the environment could be a vast warehouse with shelving up to the rafters or a flickering monitor that's slowly uploading a site developed for midnight browsing.

Focus groups and qualitative research zero in on the fuzzy, ill-conceived ideas that deserve to be tossed into the discard pile. Or they indicate which fork in the road makes the most sense. At times, your results can confirm that you're in sync with customer need. The key lies in asking the right people the right questions. If they think someone is really listening, consumers will fall over themselves to tell you the answers.

This is a guide to understanding and learning to appreciate the people out there buying your products, services, and brands. Many marketers make the mistake of seeing the consumer as prey or as an adversary. Not so. The consumer is not the enemy; the consumer is us.

As consumers ourselves, we know that there are products and services that will make our lives easier, simpler, and more comfortable and brands that will make us feel better, smarter, more confident, and attractive. The businesses that will survive in an era of killer competition and product proliferation—whether it's the dot.com or the dry cleaner—are seriously exploring how their customers think and feel about them. By listening to the consumer's voice, you can learn the true capabilities of your business.

As the pages of this book reveal, focus groups have more to do with concentrated and creative listening than with numbers and projections. If you have watched focus groups and ticked off numbers and ratings, this is not listening; it's recording. Tapes will perform that role for you.

Every qualitative analysis report has a caveat to the reader to absent the findings and hypotheses from facts, and place them instead in the realm of possibilities. The implicit warning: This information was gathered in a nonscientific manner. Don't even begin to project these findings on to any population other than the one involved in this study. Just because a handful of women in northern New Jersey reacted favorably to a proposed commercial doesn't mean that people across the United States may be expected to react favorably.

Number-counting does not have its place in qualitative research, and in that regard, findings should not be projected. However, firsthand comments from consumers about how they live their lives and what's important to them in this fast-moving society are valid. If manufacturers really care about being responsible providers of products and services, they have to heed what customers are saying about how they're feeling and how they're expressing themselves as well. Analysts can only accomplish this in a face-to-face situation where they are able to judge the intent of the speaker because they are seeing the whole person, not just looking at a string of words on a screen or making assumptions about the opinions of individuals based on cumulative data about groups.

Context provides the reality you may be missing from your other forms of market research. You can take an idea to a mall and talk to 200 passersby and know that you got a terrific "buy score" that suits the company's benchmark for further work. Now, you need to understand why the respondents answered that way, how it might fit into their current life, how they really feel (yes, emotionally) about the idea, and then judge all of this information from your own experienced and practiced perspective as a professional marketer. Whether you're marketing products and services for a billion-dollar corporation or are out peddling a start-up brand, you can find more to say, and can do a better job of selling, once you listen to your potential customer.

In corporate research presentations, I remind my clients that the analysis I'm about to share with them and the advice I'm going to leave behind is my personal and educated take on what went on and what makes sense to focus on or to ignore. I encourage clients to share their own takes on what they heard and observed and how it does or doesn't jibe with the impressions they had before listening to the panelists in focus groups. That way, we all leave better prepared to do our jobs.

I have identified the majority of my actual experiences with specific brands because I don't want my points to get lost in a sea of vague references to "major manufacturers" and "another Fortune 100 company." I have given careful thought to how much or how little to reveal about the assignments and have concluded that in most cases the brands will benefit from being mentioned. My advice to those cited, or their competitors, is this: Look to these key examples for the implications for your own business today. I hope what you learn from them will help you bring to future focus groups a more finely honed sense of how valuable focused listening can be.

Qualitative research results are impressionistic and interpretable. Like our own personal memory banks, what we remember is usually an interpretation of actual events. As Lily Tomlin says in her brilliant one-woman show: "What else is reality but an educated hunch?" These pages contain my personal impressions of what happened and why. Together with your own impressions and experiences, they can maximize your benefits from the valuable tool of focus groups.

BONNIE GOEBERT

ACKNOWLEDGMENTS

This book began by invitation.

What happened was that Ellen Geiger, literary agent par excellence at Curtis Brown and a friend of mine, was having drinks with Katherine Persky, account supervisor par excellence at Gotham Advertising and a friend of mine. Business came up and Katherine, who was then between jobs, mentioned that she had been doing some interviewing for me as part of a major worldwide hair-coloring initiative to understand how hairdressers think. The more they spoke, the more Ellen began to sense a book. This, after all, is what literary agents do.

Thanks to Ellen for calling and asking me if I'd like to write a book on my adventures in the moderating trade. This suggestion to write a book was nothing new to me. Any moderator who sits around and tells tales to clients is usually entertaining enough for people to say, "Gee, you should write a book about all this." The difference here was that Ellen is a literary agent and not a product manager. Ellen was serious. Ellen was persuasive. Ellen found the inimitable Herma M. Rosenthal to take my thoughts and put them into a readable format. Thanks, Herma.

So the book was started. Three years later, the book is complete.

What I wish is that Gene Reilly were still alive to read it. He was one of the pioneers of qualitative research, and I began my career under his dedicated and patient tutelage. When I joined the E.L. Reilly Co., Inc., on East Fifty-sixth Street in 1968, focus groups were still being challenged as a viable research methodology. Some moderators referred to focus group participants as numbers so as not to lose a sense of objectivity. Focus group facilities had observation booths that were tiny little cubicles with stools. There were no M&Ms to munch, Perrier had not yet hit the American shores, and bottled water didn't exist. Panelists were recruited without benefit of a written questionnaire.

Gene renamed the company The Gene Reilly Group, and we moved to Darien, Connecticut, in 1974. This is when focus groups and all other forms of qualitative research really took off. Gene and I were among the first moderators to use an easel in focus groups. We developed and marketed the Consumer Management Team Interaction, which uniquely placed consumers in the same room with clients to brainstorm product and advertising ideas. We fiddled around with all manner of projective exercises until we found ones that consumers could relate to and that would produce meaningful results. Thanks, Gene.

Gene not only taught me how to moderate, he taught me how to design projects, how to analyze the results, how to write, how to survive on the road, and most of all, how to listen.

B. G.

CONTENTS

1

LISTENING 101

The Value of Focus Groups

Millions say the apple fell but Newton was the one to ask why.

Bernard Baruch

In the 1950s, so the story goes, the food technologists and home economists at Betty Crocker thought they had a winner on their hands with a one-step cake mix. Just add liquid and allakazaam . . . cake batter. This was during the Eisenhower years when convenience foods and make-my-life-easier appliances were the rallying cry. The folks at Betty Crocker thought they couldn't miss. Women who bought the product and baked the cake felt otherwise.

What went wrong? To find out, I'll bet some pioneer market researchers consulted housewives. (Remember this was the 1950s. A few years later, housewives became "homemakers" because "wives" in "houses" were becoming outmoded. That, of course, begat stay-at-home-moms with a pride agenda all their own for the truly labor-intensive aspects of raising a family and maintaining a home that extend far beyond the simpler sobriquet, *housewife*. Such attitudinal changes feed the demand for my brand of qualitative research.)

The focus group leaders probably queried and questioned housewives who had used cake mixes until they finally understood where they had failed. The problem: The cake mix was a little too simple. The consumer felt no sense of accomplishment, no involvement with the product. It made her feel useless, especially if somewhere her aproned mom was still whipping up cakes from scratch.

Undaunted, the brain trust at Betty Crocker went back to work. They reformulated the mix so that along with water, the user would have to add an egg. The true accomplishment for those early marketers, however, was in ferreting out how housewives felt about using a boxed mix to make cake batter. The real answer was an insight: Put pride back in the cake-baking process.

The tale may be apocryphal, but it has been told and retold to market researchers to demonstrate a point: *If you want to know what the consumer thinks . . . ask. Then listen. And then ask again to see if you've got it right. And before you give it to them, ask and listen again.* It's why we conduct focus groups.

The focus group is an invisible part of the marketing machinery. Betty Crocker aside, it's virtually impossible to follow the breadcrumbs from a series of focus groups to a successful (or unsuccessful) marketing effort. Consumers seldom give you the solution. They do help you pinpoint the problem. My hunch is that no homemaker told Betty Crocker to put the egg in. I suspect she merely expressed a reluctance to use the mix without quite knowing why. The real problem had nothing to do with the product's intrinsic value, but instead represented the emotional connection that links a product to its user.

If you want to understand the whys and wherefores of product use . . . or discontinued product use . . . or occasional product use . . . or your brand . . . or your competitor's brand . . . focus groups are where you get the picture. They are the maternity wards and rehab clinics for brands. (Apologies to my good friend and client, futurist Faith Popcorn for borrowing her metaphor. She was the first to think of her company, Brain Reserve, as the stop-in clinic—not the full-service hospital—for Fortune 500 clients worried about a specific aspect of their business.) As a market researcher to many of those same Fortune 500 companies, my focus groups are the wellness centers where the true skill is in the diagnosis. Faith and consultants like Jack Trout are the practitioners; qualitative marketing researchers like me are the diagnosticians.

Focus groups are the ideal place to begin understanding what products mean to consumers in their deep psyches rather than their deep pockets. Dismiss the notion of someone out in a suburban mall, clipboard in hand, asking every passerby if he or she likes Pepsi better than Coke. I want to know why. Strike the idea of a screening room full of people voting to alter the end of *Fatal Attraction* so Glenn Close gets her comeuppance. I want to understand how either ending makes the audience feel.

Which do you prefer, or what do you like better are questions best handled in surveys. They fall under *quantitative* research that tells you which one, how many, how often, and by whom. But focus groups are a *qualitative* research technique that lets you dig past the measurements. If you want to know how many jelly beans are in the jar, or how many are red, yellow, orange, or pink, then quantitative is your game. If you wonder how each jelly bean tastes, or how the colors may or may not relate to flavor, then qualitative is what you need.

Qualitative research (mainly focus groups) is where a story unfolds, a hypothesis develops, and an explanation emerges. Its value rests in the ability to allow a client to understand totally a brand preference, a purchase decision, the lack of interest in a well-advertised product, or why Glenn Close needs to get hers in the end.

Of course, someone might have concluded "fuggedaboudit," the cake mix won't sell. A savvy marketer instead listened to users, developed some insights, and wondered what Betty Crocker could do to counteract an apparent sense of inadequacy. Hence, the egg.

For the past three decades, I've been listening to consumers talk about room deodorizers, potato chips, credit cards, furniture polish, cars, washing machines, bubble gum, ATMs, newspapers, breath mints, and practically any other product you can think of (never cake mixes, by the way). And, I'm constantly surprised by what they have to say. Not necessarily because the conclusions are unanticipated but because so much learning can take place when you reach beyond hard, cold figures and talk eyeball to eyeball with consumers. These are the real people who make choices about what products to buy, use them in individual ways, and become emotionally attached to the brands they prefer. It's simply a matter of full throttle and focused listening.

Why Conduct a Focus Group?

Most of us operate on automatic pilot when we drive a car. We don't stop to think about putting the key in the ignition, starting the car, or turning the steering wheel. We do it almost without thought, by habit. From going to the supermarket to reading a newspaper, we don't analyze our motivations, we simply act.

Focus groups take the "automatic" out of buying patterns and put them on manual override for a while to help you understand what's going on in your customers' psyches. By delving into the consumers' consciousness you can unearth the underlying reasons for their actions and form reasoned impressions about what's really going on.

A simple survey will only identify which brand of aspirin, ibuprofen (most consumers just call it all "Advil"), or acetaminophen (and they call all this "Tylenol") consumers buy. What you won't find out is what goes through any consumer's mind when he's in a drug store standing in front of that shelf. You could set up a video camera and tape him at the scene. I think you get more useful information if you just ask. That's when you'll hear: "It's so confusing now. There's aspirin and Advil and Tylenol. But, what's Aleve? Then there's gel caps and tablets. And this brand mentions headaches, that one says muscle pain, and here's one that suggests it will work for fevers." Listen to him. What he's wondering is what's going to relieve his wife's tennis elbow, which is why he's standing bewildered at the shelf in the first place.

Just listen to consumers talk about the analgesics area of mass retail outlets, with nary a pharmacist in sight. And bend a little closer when those over 50, with less than perfect vision and arms that can't reach far enough, tell you the frustration of not being able to get an item off the shelf or read the miniscule print on the label that might actually shed some light on which brand of analgesic to purchase.

You may have all the data but you haven't heard what consumers are really saying, which is that the proliferation of similar painkillers is driving them nuts. And, if they can't find what they want in the supermarket within 30 seconds they'll just grab whatever is in easy reach, pay the asking price, and go about their business.

Surveys and focus groups shouldn't be mutually exclusive. I would never advise any client to conduct a set of focus groups in place of a statistically sophisticated survey. Marketers today need all the data they can get, and they need to be able to view any form of market research with impunity.

What qualitative research does is add depth and context. Would the results be exactly the same if you spoke to another group of 10 people? Maybe not. Unlike quantitative research, qualitative doesn't have the statistical accuracy of a survey. Focus groups are only one weapon in the arsenal of research tools that marketers use.

Often, when I tell people what I do for a living, they expect me to make an instant connection between their favorite commercial and the group of people who gave it thumbs up, or they'll present their own interpretation of focus groups: "You show new products to consumers and see how they feel about them, right?"

Focus groups have significantly less to do with gathering new product reactions than with understanding what a new product should look like, feel like, smell like, and ultimately promise the customer. Hardly anyone advances a business proposition or a new product or service based on a gut feel. The stakes are just too high.

Focus groups are an important market research tool if you are ready to listen. Don't expect answers. Don't expect solutions. Go in prepared to hear what you haven't thought about before. Usually, a good round of focus groups gives rise to more questions, but they will be more precise.

Listening in focus groups is like painting. Each panelist and each group adds color and texture. In the end, a cohesive picture should and usually does emerge. Focus groups work best for the following tasks:

- *To explore customers' purchasing habits.*
  Why are they buying your mustard brand . . . or your competitor's? Why are consumers purchasing low-salt items in some food categories like snacks and not others? Why aren't they visiting your Web site even though they seem to be aware of it? Why do women drop in and out of hair-coloring products?

- *To understand more about the particular consumer in the category.*
  You want to launch a product targeted to pet owners. To determine if the concept will fly, first you need to know how those consumers view and treat their pets. Why do they anthropomorphize their pets? How do they talk about their pets? Is there a difference between dog and cat owners, owners of small animals versus large animals, owners of purebred versus mixed breeds?

- *To learn more about consumers' attitudes.*
  As a low-fat product marketer, you're interested in the attitudes of people who are and aren't watching their weight. What are the differences between those who buy the product for their families and those who purchase it just for themselves?

- *To examine a brand's image.*
  How do people view your coffee? Are you hip moccacino grande or yesterday's tired instant? Does your potential customer see your men's store as discomfiting as a snake pit or as comfy as an old shoe?

- *To discern consumers' emotional bonds with a product.*
  Your cleaning product costs less and seems to do a better job than your competitor's, yet customers consistently buy

the competition—why? Is it because it's the brand their mothers used or does it make users feel that they're smarter?

- *To develop an effective advertising campaign.*
  Women might color their hair because they believe it makes them look as young as they feel, but do they really want to hear that in the advertising? Is it better to stress that your fast food is quick and convenient or that it tastes great?

- *To feed an educated hunch.*
  You've developed a hypothesis about why people in upper income brackets might use your new financial service. How do you know if your conclusion is right?

The insights that emerge from all this prodding and probing can help marketers refine their products and services, define the core customers most receptive to them, and reach and retain those consumers with relevant and appropriate messages.

LISTENING POINTS

- Ask consumers what they think before you assume you know what they need.
- Use surveys to find out when, how many, or how often; use focus groups to find out why.
- Listen hard for opportunity; sometimes it knocks softly.
- Focus groups don't provide solutions. They help you form a picture that reveals your possibilities and limits.
- A good focus group will yield better questions, not definitive answers.

2

CHOOSING THE VOICES

Who Should—And Shouldn't—Be in Focus Groups

When I first got into this field, I was writing a report about the results of a hand lotion survey and having a heck of a time trying to figure out what was going on. I was staring at statistical tables with little boxes representing age groups—women 18 to 25, women 26 to 34, and so on—and I had a massive computer print-out of data. (This was before we could access data on a screen.)

The information indicated that women in Phoenix liked the product better than women in Chicago. I thought perhaps people in dry climates liked the lotion's creamy feel while the women braving icy cold weather didn't want to put sticky hands in their gloves and mittens. I wondered if the lotion tested in the Southwest market was called Desert Flower and the one for the Midwest was called Hand Guard, would that have altered their feelings about the product? Would women with dishwashers have a different per-spective than those who washed cups and saucers by hand?

All I was expected to conclude was that more women 18 to 25 in Phoenix preferred lotion number 102 than the same age group in Chicago. It scored really well on not leaving behind a greasy residue, but really low on fragrance. Just fill in the cells. Although I trusted the findings, as a fledgling qualitative researcher I wanted to know more. I was looking for the "why." Since I couldn't see or speak—or listen—directly to the people who had participated in this study, I began to form my own hypotheses.

The client called and asked that I be removed from the account immediately. Admittedly, I went too far in trying to examine the psyches of desert dwellers versus cold clime inhabitants, but I was on the right track. Those cells existed only on paper. The box labeled 18 to 25 in fact represented people with a wide span of attitudes and feelings, prejudices and preferences, employed, unemployed, singles, parents, professionals—real, whole people. In marketing, you have to look at complete human beings and the best way to do that is to sit down and talk face to face with a carefully selected group of people.

Since it costs companies approximately $500 a panelist to conduct a focus group, you want to talk to people who will give you the most bang for the buck. Who's going to provide the most useful information? Perhaps equally important, whom should you exclude? You don't want anyone sitting in that chair who might unknowingly throw a monkey wrench into the works because of his or her rigid attitude or behavior. You can learn little from such consumers, and there's less you can do to change them. Consumer attitude drives product usage.

Background Check

When a company like Stouffer's is trying to gauge reaction to a new gourmet frozen food idea, they may immediately think about women with families who prepare the evening meal. That's fine if you're out taking a survey of 500 people. I'm sitting down with a few groups of at most 10 people. It's like planning a dinner party; there's an optimum number and mix that ensure lively conversation and a convivial atmosphere. As I think about the invitees, my primary consideration is who will provide the most insightful information for my client; my first thoughts run to those cooks I *don't* want in that room. The mother whose menu is limited to what her children will eat (macaroni and cheese and chicken fingers seven nights a week) won't cut it. Out go the people who never try new food, who are Kosher, who have food allergies, who are professional chefs. All of that background information has to be considered. A packaged goods manufacturer like Stouffer's probably doesn't want to hear from the health-food shopper who's going to focus on artificial ingredients, salt, fat, and carbos. I want to know how someone who regularly uses the product category plans dinner menus before I let the person sit in that $500 chair.

Even the best of recruiting intentions can go awry. I conducted several groups for Playtex as they tried to come up with a great new panty for women. Playtex intended to charge a premium for a really great pair of underpants, so they wanted us to be sure that we recruited women who were spending upward of $8 for each pair of panties. Since women may *think* that they buy a specific brand (when actually they don't) and have paid a certain amount (when they didn't), to be on the safe side, we asked our recruits how much they usually spent, and then as a precaution, asked them to bring in the label from a pair of their panties so that we could verify the cost.

During the recruiting process, someone must have mixed up her antecedents. The instruction to "cut the label out of your underpants, and be sure to bring it to the group" resulted in this action: At least two panelists showed up with panties in their purses. Each pair of panties had the label neatly cut out.

We're busy and may listen with half an ear. Not only are panelists likely to bring their underwear to groups, but they honestly may think they are using products that they're not. The proliferation of products increases that prospect, making recruiting the right panelists a process bordering on badgering.

I recently did a toothpaste study, and we wanted to be sure that we weren't getting anybody who used Colgate Total. It was okay if it was Colgate Whitener, or Colgate for Sensitive Teeth, or Colgate Gel or Paste, but not Colgate Total. We asked our recruits once, then called to make certain, then called a third time and had them check the tube, then asked them when they showed up at the group to bring the tube of Colgate they did use. Because of that rigor, it then took me 30 minutes to de-intimidate the consumers in the group and convince them that "all answers are right."

It's not enough to know that someone purchases the product. When I first began doing work for Reckitt & Colman (now Reckitt Benckiser), the global king of niche cleaning products like Easy-Off, as well as power brands like Lysol, we didn't screen out people who had cleaning help. The women who participated had all the right products under the sink. They bought them, they just didn't know anything about them. A little wiser, we amended the screening questionnaire (the device we use to qualify people for focus groups), by asking: "Are you, or is someone else, personally responsible for cleaning your home?"

All panelists are not created equal. In the mid 1990s, Maxwell House was interested in talking to Generation X about a new coffee beverage they were hoping to launch. In their minds, everybody 18 to 26 was like a cast member of *Friends*, hip and hanging out in coffee houses. Then they started to hear 23-year-old guys, married with children, who sounded more like baby boomers. Well why not? Despite his tender age, even a 23-year-old may take on a different persona given the responsibilities of family and fatherhood.

As Internet investing was beginning to take off, I was doing research for a projected financial advisory service from American Express. We decided to speak to people who had portfolios of more than $200,000 and invested via different methodologies (i.e., full service or discount brokers, financial advisers, banks, and online). We expected the Internet users to be hotshot trader types. Half of them were; the other half were people who confessed they knew so little about the stock market that they were embarrassed to consult with a broker. Internet investing allowed them anonymity. They didn't have to rationalize their pick to a broker, who might dismiss the choice as foolhardy.

Once again, we thought we had an audience that seemed to get along with each other because they fit certain demographic criteria, but in actuality, their attitudes toward life, toward each other, toward money, toward products, services, and brands were outside the demographic realm. It was a repeat version of the 23-year-old guy who was changing diapers rather than coffee filters.

We learned much more when we separated these online investors by attitude instead of by behavior; for example, "insecure neophytes" versus "sophisticated investors." Working within a homogenized structure in focus groups enhanced our ability to discern and classify what people were saying and hence how to reach them. In contrast, when all the panelists in the group qualified mainly because they *behaved* similarly—they had all invested in a similar manner—we were unable to get a clear focus on a viable positioning since their outlooks and needs continued to be in sharp contrast.

I distinctly remember talking to one group in Chicago with stock portfolios in excess of $200,000. I felt like a crisis manager as I tried to explain to the woman who had just inherited her fortune that her naiveté was as important for me to understand as was the perspective of the day trader across the table. We even had someone who had won a state lottery. Their attitudes toward the concepts were being radically and understandably affected by their attitudes toward investing.

Once we segmented by those attitudes toward investing, the idea that jumped out was that the unsure trader sought a reassuring arm around her shoulder. American Express might be able to snare a big piece of the action with the novice investor by building on the brand's established financial adviser cachet. The company had nothing to gain by competing with the E-Trades or Schwabs of the early online investing world who execute orders within minutes but as discount brokers offer no coddling.

Eliminate the Negative

I loathe and detest one of the big three long distance providers. No matter how many times they call and how many low-priced multi-minute long distance and/or local deals they offer, the moment I hear the name, I hang up. If a competitor, even one I'm rather lukewarm about, phones with a promotion, I'll spend a polite amount of time listening. My distaste for this brand is totally irrational, I know; but avoiding this kind of unmanageable and unalterable negativity is especially important when you are choosing panelists. You need to be certain that people you're talking to are open-minded and won't balk at new ideas and services primarily out of an irrational aversion to the brand.

Phone companies, other utilities, and banks all seem to engender intense negative reaction. I've worked on several projects for American Express, and there are people whose veins instantly pop at the mere mention of the brand. Whether they think it's unfair to charge a fee or had a dispute about a charge—whatever the reason—bashers take everyone else down with them. Chalk them up as a lost cause and concentrate on those with a more tolerant view. If people abhor American Express — or Visa or Discover — they're not interested in anything that's coming from that brand, no matter how wonderful it seems.

Kids Don't Say the Darnedest Things

High School Students

Unless I'm trying to ferret out information for a product or idea aimed strictly at kids and teenagers, I try to avoid doing groups with them. It's just too tough squeezing useful information out of adolescents. If you have a teen, you know that "nothing" and "I don't know" are the responses to 99 percent of your questions. Blank stares and single-syllable retorts greet questions like "Why do you use Herbal Essence shampoo?" or "What does Noxzema do for your skin?" But I would bet almost anything that when they're alone, they're saying: "I love the smell of Noxzema. I want my face to be as tight as possible. I'm going to get that zit." Or, "The mechanic who fixes the car in the Herbal Essence ad is sooooo cute."

If I could go down the elevator or into the bathroom with teenage girls, I'm sure I'd walk away hearing it all. But since there are no one-way mirrors in public lavatories or elevators . . . yet, what we do with children and teenagers is respect some fundamental kid things.

Even though the market might be 13- to 18-year-olds, we never ever, ever, ever put them all in the same room. That 13-year-old who's just edged out of her horse fetish in favor of wanting to be Britney Spears is simply not going to mesh with the 17-year-old who's thinking about how she'll get the car for her Friday date. This is our rule of thumb: Put high school classmates together; junior and seniors get on great even though the age span might be 15 to 18; and freshmen and sophomores relate well to each other.

There are a few more elements to keep in mind when you're out to learn from teens. Make every effort to recruit kids who are actively involved in extracurricular activities. You're more likely to have a fighting chance of getting them to open up if they have a job, are on a school team, participate in church groups or work on school newspapers. Any group activity (with the possible exception of gang membership) will increase the odds of a more articulate youngster. We can all remember the severe peer pressure of teenage years. It may have persuaded us to smoke, dress in ridiculous garb, and ignore that in striving for independence from adults, we would go to any extreme to be totally dependent on those in our peer group. Peer pressure can be especially potent in focus groups if the panelists know each other, are falling over each other to sound alike, and don't want to disagree on anything. Deep down they know that they don't like the smell of Noxzema, but a good friend might love it.

I try to get representation from as many schools as possible. I usually don't allow any more than two students from the same school, and hope they're not best friends who will whisper to each other throughout the groups. You're never going to understand all of the dynamics of high school life in a couple of hours, but when teenagers are just meeting for the first time, there's no established hierarchy. There's a greater likelihood that they will act like individuals rather than like sheep.

College Students

When organizing focus groups with college students, I usually advise my clients to forget about freshmen, unless they are going to target them while they're seniors in high school, and college seniors, unless they are seeing them as young adults.

I learned this particular lesson while doing credit card work for Citibank. If you haven't been in school for over 10 years, you would be amazed to see the strenuous, targeted, rigorous, and calculated one-on-one marketing that takes place on college campuses during September. In the quads, marketers of everything from mouthwash to Volkswagens line up with their best and most tempting offers, hoping to woo students. The gauntlet of buying opportunities rivals a Casbah.

Each brand has its own promotional gimcracks to entice and snare potential buyers, from disposable pens to yellow highlighters, from book bags to CDs, from T-shirts to travel offers.

Citibank came along and was more interested in analyzing the college market than in finding out what kind of freebie to offer. This powerful financial institution realized that if they took the time to listen to these students, they might be able to develop a relevant brand value proposition that would win their credit card loyalty. But first, they had to understand how college students felt about credit, credit cards, money, and spending, as well as about Visa versus MasterCard versus Discover versus American Express as the plastic card of choice.

At first, we simply gathered up college students according to the high school formula—freshmen and sophomores together, juniors with seniors. Big mistake. The freshmen were so naive and wide-eyed at being away from home and on their own, so overwhelmed by the academics of it all, as well as tantalized by the come-hither cries of the marketing kiosks, that it was like talking to children. They didn't have enough experience at being college students to be college students.

At the other end of the spectrum, seniors had been there, done that, and wanted out. They had survived APRs and limited credit lines and were after bigger game. They were beginning to wonder about balance transfers and accumulating mileage points.

The results from these groups were difficult to sort through. The college frosh was quickly dismissed by the second-year student for her lack of knowledge about grace periods and APRs. The seniors sounded like bankers and venture capitalists while the juniors were into buying a really great stereo system.

We smartened up. In subsequent groups, we focused on sophomores and juniors, developing meaningful insights into the emotional benefits of credit card ownership and usage and how Citibank could stand out from the kiosk crowds with a well-executed positioning rather than a soon-to-be-forgotten T-shirt.

For the college market, credit cards represented freedom, and Visa was fast bounding to the top of the heap as the brand most relevant and meaningful to these students because it was promising to "get you where you want to go." More importantly, we learned that in the dawning years of brand loyalty, appealing to the college market was extremely important for credit card providers. Think about your own habits. I'll bet that one of the credit cards that you simply can't get out of your wallet is one that you got while you were at college.

Young Children

For really little kids, it is best to use focus groups as observational opportunities. You probably can't talk to anyone under the age of 4, but you can observe behavior. I did a project for Gillette, which had invented a new packaging for disposable razors (imagine a razor in an orange-juice can). The government has strict rules about the packaging of dangerous items like razors. Gillette had to prove that they had done their homework and made the product tamperproof for young kids.

We put the rug-rat set in a room with a lot of these packages and simply watched how they went about trying to open them.

(This same technique probably gave rise to all those frustrating "childproof" medicine vials. But don't blame me. I didn't do that research.) Anyhow, the kids were supposed to first go after it on their own; then we instructed them to really try to get it open. Finally we told them to use whatever means necessary. They could use their teeth; they could stomp on it; they could throw it around.

Despite wonderfully valiant attempts, the children were unable to open the can via any manipulation, and Gillette felt confident about using the packaging. Only it never did. Why is another story, but next time you're struggling with a tamperproof anything, know that the manufacturer probably spent a few bucks assuring that it wouldn't be easy for preschoolers to get at.

Child and teen qualitative research is best left in the hands of the experts. Things change so rapidly that unless you're always talking to the child market, you can quickly lose sight of what's in and what's out. As of this writing, children were lining up for the next Harry Potter book. By the time you read this book, Harry Potter may be out, out, out, and ridiculous.

In understanding any type of consumer behavior, it's important to be familiar with the spheres of influence; if I don't know kids' reference points, I can't effectively analyze what they're saying and do a good job of advising my clients. The older the kid, the longer the sphere of influence is apt to exist. I'm confident that I know what's happening in the college market. I'm on shaky ground as the age limit drops.

Opposites Don't Attract

Do you keep an opened jar of mustard in the pantry or the refrigerator? Whichever you do, I'm here to tell you that a large percentage of people in this country do exactly the opposite. Put individuals at extreme ends of the behavioral/attitudinal spectrum together in the same room and you need to wear a striped shirt and carry a whistle.

Before smoking was banned in most public places, I did a job testing new shampoo concepts for Clairol. By chance, one group in San Francisco turned out to have an equal number of smokers and nonsmokers. That essential difference became apparent while they were waiting for the focus group to start. Once it did, it was like watching the Sharks and the Jets. Any concept that the smokers really liked, nonsmokers despised . . . on principle.

When Sterno, that little can of stuff you light under chafing dishes to keep food warm, was looking to expand into new products, we decided to talk to women who entertained at least twice a month for people other than family. We were conducting the groups in an upmarket area of Connecticut and wanted to make sure that our panelists would represent a broad income spectrum. They did, but to our unthinking dismay, we got oil and water. On one side were five women who entertained with china, crystal, and linen, and on the other, five who would just as soon use paper and plastic. Half were interested in a product that wouldn't tarnish silver, while the others were looking for one that didn't attract mosquitoes. The concepts got buried because the discussion degenerated into class warfare.

Age Matters

You can mix generations as long as it's in a category where age doesn't really matter. A 25-year-old and a 55-year-old can probably engage in amiable discourse about Frank's Hot Sauce. People who love spicy food will bond over the thermonuclear power of their favorite burn-inducing condiment.

Change the subject to skin care and you're into a whole different dynamic. The 20-year-old woman combs the shelves for a moisturizer that's inexpensive, because she's doesn't have a lot of money to spend on it, and that isn't too creamy, because she's still worried about zits. She looks for a product with an astringent quality. The middle-aged woman looks in the mirror hoping she won't find a new wrinkle. Any alcohol-based unguent is the enemy of her dry skin. Hydration is her savior. If she believes a product will keep the calendar on hold, price takes a back seat. After all, it's cheaper than the surgeon's knife. Each generation has valid needs, they're simply not interested in those differences when they're in the same room.

Gender Bender

Conventional wisdom used to hold that it was a bad idea to mix men and women in the same group because the men would overshadow the women. Times have changed. Today, women have much more to say about areas that 20 years ago were thought of as strictly testosterone territory. In mixed groups, more often than not I have to interrupt the women to let the guys speak. Men are so used to being bashed that they sit there totally intimidated.

Women tend to be far more knowledgeable about taking advantage of credit cards than men. When you put the two together in a group, women can chatter incessantly about credit card use; they'll know what bank a card is affiliated with, their credit limit, how many points they'll accrue, and in what circumstances they use each card.

It's a whole other story with men. More than likely, they'll carry just one (maybe the card they got in college), and unless they take it out of their wallet, won't know if it's Visa or Master-Card. If it's not a major bank, like Citibank, they won't have any idea who issued it and when it comes to paying the bill, married guys are apt to tell you their wives handle it.

Women are great at helping you improve an idea. Men will say that's a wonderful idea—or it stinks. Women will talk in detail and with specifics to make it better. Men are more broad stroke and general. Love it or hate it, they want to take the rest of the time making sure that whatever the product, it's being marketed to the right audience in the right venue. "Why not get a commercial on Super Bowl?" Right!

I did sessions for Teflon in its quest to come up with new product ideas beyond building wrap and omelet pans. Among a host of wonderful properties, Teflon's major feature is that it acts as a lubricant; it ensures that things won't stick, makes them easier to clean, and makes products work faster. One guy came up with the idea to use Teflon in TV remote controls so that surfing would be even easier; the session hit a standstill as the rest of the male panelists signed on to his brilliance.

In work for Nu Skin, a direct marketer of skin care products, we had a wealth of new concepts to get early feedback on. Most of the ideas were for women, but in an effort to expand their market, Nu Skin realized that the contemporary male was getting more and more vain about his skin and appearance. It wasn't unreasonable to think he might want to go beyond the morning shave.

One moisturizing toner being considered had appeal for both sexes. As women discussed it, they became excited, got into its potential fragrance and consistency; whether it would be sufficiently non-drying, how best to package it, and how they wanted it to feel on their faces. They used understandable examples of what the product should be like when they smoothed it on their skin.

Men were equally thrilled with the idea. Only they kept stressing what a great marketing strategy it would be to sell the moisturizer through barbers.

LISTENING POINTS

◉ Who should not be in a focus group is as important as who should be included.

◉ Consumers often don't listen any better than marketers.

◉ Beware of brand bashers. They'll bring everyone else down to their level.

◉ Avoid polar opposites in focus groups. Strive for homogenization in the broad bell curve.

◉ Use behavioral similarities to develop hunches about attitudinal differences.

◉ Listen to differentiated attitudinal segments to refine your hunches.

◉ Understand the reference points of any group you listen to.

3

LISTENING BEHIND THE MIRROR

Who Should Be Listening

Advertisers and marketers spend more than a billion dollars a year to delve into the motivations and habits of consumers. They watch behind the one-way mirror, nervously munching on M&Ms or crudités, gulping down oceans of designer water, hoping panelists will warmly accept their concept or product, dying a little each time they don't. What does she like about my idea? How does he feel about my brand versus the competition? What about my ad is really working with the consumer? How can it have more impact? In a world cluttered with ever more products and information, how can mine stand out?

Painters often take a portrait off the easel, turn it around and look at it in the mirror. When they see the reflection, they suddenly realize the nose is too large and the ears are too square and the eyes are too wide. Likewise, focus groups provide marketers with a sharper image of their brands and a keener sense of their limitations and their possibilities. The companies that listen to consumers even if they don't always like what they hear—that listen to the simple as well as complex truths and then try to adjust—realize that it's considerably less work, less effort, and less expensive to change their product than to attempt changing the consumer. The peculiar aspect of all this is how many companies disregard or fail to act on the information they've spent all this money to get.

We Are All Consumers

The prevailing assumption is that you have to be manipulative to sell stuff. Fly under the consumers' radar, catch them unaware and then trap them into buying your product. It's war, a matter of stealth and deception. Many marketers operate under the misconception that they not only are smarter than their quarry—the customers—but are above the same ploys. They conveniently overlook their role as the target when they shop for their Rolexes, BMWs, and Prada bags.

The consuming world is not divided into us and them. As consumers, we all share an emotional attachment to the brands we buy. It's not just a matter of taste that pushes us to put Tropicana in the cart over Minute Maid, buy Lancôme lipstick at a department store versus Maybelline at the drug store, drive a Volvo sedan instead of a Lincoln Continental.

Part of what focus groups should accomplish is to take the blinders off clients so they can see buyers as whole people, not just the end point on a decision tree about salad dressing choices. The consumer isn't a faceless blob sprawled out on a couch waiting for marching orders. With a deeper understanding of the entire human being, marketers can fine-tune their message, make advertising more relevant and products more meaningful. They can connect with their customers rather than produce marketing campaigns that seem designed to impress their colleagues in the adjoining cubicle.

Coming out from behind the Mirror

For brainstorming sessions, I like to put the clients and consumers in the same room because it encourages spontaneous and real-time building on ideas. Clients listen more intently when they're sitting next to someone rather than observing them from behind a thick slab of one-way mirror. It knocks out complacency, the ideas are richer than when just clients are involved in an off-site to blue sky and there's no consumers in the immediate vicinity to add a note of reality. By that same token, consumers don't really care about having new products developed (there are too many to pick from already) and need the stimulation of the real client in the room to stay with the order of the day.

Clients are apt to see that one-way mirror as a wall that protects them from their customers. In some instances, it becomes clients' last refuge against reality. I was doing sessions with principals from a new dot.com company, one of whom asked me if he should wait until the group started before going to the bathroom, which was located across from the waiting room. Why? He didn't want any of the panelists to see him. In truth, no one would have known who he was, but advertisers and marketers cling to a deep-seated fear of confronting the people who might buy and use their stuff.

That's why I wasn't surprised to be greeted with a minute of incredulous silence after telling another client hoping to come up with new ideas for his product that I planned to put his managers in the same room with consumers. When we finally did the creativity sessions with consumers and clients together, this same executive was sitting next to a woman who was a loyal user of his brand, and the two were bonding over having teenage daughters who had gotten over bouts with anorexia. As the session progressed, they were building off each other's ideas. The category, incidentally, wasn't even vaguely related to food, teenagers, or drugs for depression. It was for new toilet bowl cleaners.

Regardless of the category, the ideas are usually better when marketers interact with their customers and really hear them. If your strategic thinking never gets above putting one over on consumers, you're going to feel mighty uncomfortable sitting across the table from them. It's a mistake to view consumers as fish waiting to be reeled in. They'll only take that bait once. But if you're willing to see them as members of the team, then you should be eager to face off to find solutions.

Who's Buying Your Product?

Brand marketers frequently come in armed with preconceived notions about who their consumers are, and then they're shocked when the real thing greets them. Consumers are not recruited from central casting. As in most areas of life, an open mind yields the most insightful learning.

In the late 1970s, somebody put together a combination of characteristics, slapped it with an acronym, and yuppies were born. Clients were streaming in from all over the world to New York, Los Angeles, San Francisco, and Chicago to see Yuppies up close. A well-known Scotch distiller took all these characteristics, thought of all the questions to search out the people who had them, and asked us to conduct groups in New York. People showed up: Some of them were not White, several weren't slender, and a few were not especially articulate. But they were *young*, they were *urban*, they were *professional*, and they were drinking my client's brand of Scotch. Attitudinally, they cared about all the things that yuppies care about. They were impressed by the status of that brand and were highly aspirational.

My client protested, arguing that these were not the young urban professionals he had in mind. "Well, they really are," I assured him. "Look at that heavyset woman over there. She's a vice president in a major corporation. This Hispanic man works on Wall Street as a trader." But they didn't fit the part. They weren't the white-skinned, white-collar, white-bread version in power suits and stiletto heels that he had in mind. Perhaps with foresight, he might have recognized an opportunity to make inroads with his brand through a policy of inclusion.

Taking a Step Back

I worked with a woman at Colgate who had been in charge of the marketing of a product called Fresh Start. It was a blue detergent that had little granules that would bounce rather than form clumps like a powder. It came in a nice sexy plastic container and was supposed to attract a more upscale buyer. The first time she saw Fresh Start on the shelf, she ran up to it, embraced the package and had her fiancé take a picture of her standing next to the shelf.

Marketers live and breathe their products on a daily basis. The tiniest hiccup in sales can have a tidal-wave effect in a category like laundry detergents. They become so wrapped up in pushing the brand that they forget that consumers aren't operating at the same intensity. In their fantasy, from the time Jane Q. Public wakes up in the morning until bedtime at night, she is mulling over whether to choose All or Tide with Bleach Alternative.

Nor is the consumer splitting hairs about shades of meaning. Shake 'n Bake was concerned about whether to say their chicken coating was crunchy or crispy in one of their ads. If the commercial had said, "Now you can have crispy chicken," the consumer was not going to stand in protest and say: "I want my chicken crunchy, not crispy. I'm not going to buy your packaged bread crumbs." Marketers' decisions are like the choices parents must make about battles with their children. It's not worth yelling at a child for playing with his food. Save it for playing with fire.

Ironically, as close as they are to the fortunes of their brand, marketers—particularly those involved in mass-marketed packaged goods—more than likely aren't actually using them. Living in cosmopolitan urban areas on the East and West Coasts, they're just plain removed from the mall and giant supermarket culture. That's why I love to educate clients and let them hear how actual consumers use products. This feedback is usually very different from how clients, sitting at their computers reading reams and reams of data about what's selling where, perceive how real people live their lives and use their products. Marketing executives understand marketing and market share: Individual customers seem to be beyond their comprehension.

Positive Impressions

Often marketers react dismissively to consumers' comments. If they hear something that they've heard before, rather than saying, "Isn't that interesting; it confirms what we're thinking, maybe there's a trend here," they'll respond, "Oh, we knew all that before. We didn't learn anything new." If something outside the lines comes up, sometimes the very same client will say: "We never heard that before. What do eight people know?" Behind consumers' thoughts lies an implication or an insight. Their conclusions could point to a new fad or they may represent a fluke. Either way, it's all valid and possibly significant information for the marketers.

Language Barrier

George Bernard Shaw commented, "England and America are two countries separated by the same language." The same could be said for marketers and consumers. Most professions have a particular jargon that serves both as a shorthand and as a way to separate the layperson from the pro. That's exactly the problem. Inside terminology perpetuates a mind-set that distances marketers from shoppers. We call it Dijon mustard; in marketingspeak, it's a premium edible. A tampon becomes a digital insertion device; a cheese puff, an air-extruded snack. Cleaning products are divided into trigger sprays and pourables, but they're all APCs (all-purpose cleaners) to the marketer. To get into the consumer's mind, marketers have to try harder to think—and speak—in the consumer's language.

The Focus Group Is Not an Idea

When clients use focus groups like a verb—"Let's focus-group it"—it's usually a synonym for "We don't have the slightest idea of what to do. We've hit a wall." What they're saying is *maybe the consumer will tell us*, or *maybe it won't come out of the consumer's mouth, but if we get the moderator maybe she'll help us out of this dilemma because if the consumer says it, the moderator can say well this is what the consumers said, and then we the marketing people can justify why we said it should be crispy.*

The consumer is only expert at being a consumer. The consumer is not expert at writing copy, designing ads, or inventing products.

LISTENING POINTS

◎ Consumers are us.

◎ Interacting with your consumers can yield valuable insights.

◎ Come in with an open mind. You're there to listen and learn, not to listen and then to criticize.

◎ Your intended customer isn't as invested in a product as you are.

◎ Listen even if you don't like what you hear or you think you've heard it before.

◎ Avoid getting lost in the jargon you've created to sell your product.

◎ Use focus groups to explore, expand, and evaluate ideas and concepts rather than to provide the idea itself.

4

LISTENING OVER THE FENCE

The Moderator's Role

The focus group rests on the deceptively simple premise that consumers can impart valuable information. Bringing it to light is a far more delicate matter. The moderator strives to uncover the roots, conscious or not, behind consumer behavior without exerting undue influence over the process.

While the conclusions from session to session may be consistent, each group takes on a unique personality, its own dynamic and chemistry. A well-conducted focus group depends on the interaction among the participants, with the moderator (like our dinner party hostess) directing the activities, encouraging participation, and keeping the discussion moving and on target while trying to remain in the background.

If you can put people at ease and gain their trust, they can't wait to give you their opinions. Most quickly forget that ad agency representatives as well as marketing and management executives may be anxiously scrutinizing the process on the other side of the mirror. Consumers have been ranting and railing at the tube, at the newspaper, at the grocery shelf, for years. Now, finally, someone is listening.

The response that just tumbles out tends to be more revealing than the answer that is carefully thought out. I try to eliminate the filter between what's in people's brains and what comes out of their mouths. I don't want panelists censoring an answer because they don't think that's what I'm after. Besides, not every purchase decision can undergo rigorous analysis. The more you ask, for example, "Why did you buy Country Time lemonade?" the less valid will be the answer. By the fifth time you ask, "Is there any other reason why you bought it?" the panelists are lying.

Beyond just collecting opinions, the moderator interprets what it all may mean and where it might lead. In the end, the moderator forms educated guesses based on experience, context, and intuition. The consumer message isn't the holy grail, but as marketers, you ignore it at your peril. Fail to listen to and address buyers' concerns and you had better increase your shelf life because chances are that's where your product will remain.

Sometimes I'll notice a commercial or new packaging and I can track the genesis back to conclusions that were probably drawn from listening to consumers. More often, the information gleaned from a focus group disappears into the corporate fog. Surveys say that at least 90 percent of campaign directions and product possibilities just peter out, unable to jump the hurdles of corporate bureaucracy. Everybody is terribly enthusiastic at the time of the focus group, but then reality charges in. Maybe the CEO was never behind the idea to begin with. Perhaps there's a new marketing team on board. Or by the time the product reaches the upper levels, it's been through so many hands and iterations that it's unrecognizable. Or the advertising agency says that the winning commercial is going to cost $8 million because they have to produce the ad in Barbados in February to meet the deadline to be out there by May, and all the agency people have to live in first-class hotels. The hot concept cools down, replaced by the idea du jour.

Somebody once asked me what I like best about being a moderator. It's the entertainment value. The one-way mirror is a little like a proscenium arch. Part of the reward is the exuberance I feel in front of the mirror when things are going well or the anxiety when they aren't going the way the client—and I— thought they might.

The kiss of acceptance for an idea is when panelists take me aside as they're putting on their coats and say: "I can't believe two hours has gone by. When is this product going to be out? What will it be called? How will I know it?" That's heaven.

It's Not Always What They Say

Listening is believing. And part of listening is noticing. A skilled moderator will wait and watch as well as talk and hear. The roll of the eyes, the nod of the head, the doodling on the pad, absolutely everything can have meaning and significance. It's essential to be aware of every behavioral signal from the moment you greet focus group panelists until the time you thank them for having participated. How are they seating themselves . . . at a power position across from you or in a place to hide? Is someone trying to monopolize the conversation? What about the panel member who isn't venturing any opinion? If everybody is silently nodding in agreement about something and one individual's head is not moving, 9 times out of 10, that person has another perspective on the subject. Are they giving answers just to please you or perhaps that attractive panelist next to you?

When you're in a group, all of your little social antennae go up. As a panelist, you're responding to the fact that the man next to you has a tiny stain on his tie; the one to the right has crossed eyes; and the panelist across from you is beautiful, and you're captivated and jealous at the same time. You're struggling to make ends meet, and the woman over there has told you she's putting in a swimming pool and just got back from a vacation in Bermuda. The moderator has to get rid of all this extraneous stuff and help people focus on her client's area of interest without letting them realize that's what they're doing. And they have to feel good about dropping their guard.

Leading by Indirection

I just let people talk. I'm interested in what comes out of their mouths and how it comes out. I trust their words delivered casually more than formal question-and-answer sessions. "Why do you use Altoids?" will get you an answer. "Tell me about anything you put in your mouth during the day and let's say the rule is that it can't be part of a meal. Maybe you chew it, maybe you suck it, and I'm not interested in chocolate" will get you enlightenment. They're going to tell you the truth about what they use and don't use until you come in and give the group a hint about what you're really looking to talk about.

The moderator is a bit like a puppeteer, controlling the action, yet hoping panelists don't see her pulling the strings. The idea is to cover the territory without asking questions that will prejudice the outcome. An Internet company, Commerceinc.com (now one of the used-to-be's of the dot.com business-to-business frenzy) was coming out with a new b-to-b venture they wanted to call PIPE9, but they were concerned that the name might be construed as pornographic or off-color. We showed panelists three possible company names and asked them to write down what first came to mind as they saw each name and the type of enterprise they would associate with it. In this unaided exercise, porno never came up for the PIPE9 name.

Okay. Then we aided the panel by presenting a broad concept for an Internet business-to-business company and discussed which of the three names fit and suggested possible imagery for this business. For the PIPE9 name, most panelists keyed in on b-to-b channeling and a few said that the name was a bit likely to indicate a surfing and skateboarding Web site. Importantly, nothing with sexual content was mentioned.

Finally, at the end of the session just to double-check, I prompted them, asking point-blank if there was anything at all that was suggestive about the name. Nope. Had I planted the seed in their minds at the beginning of the session by asking, "Does the name PIPE9 sound pornographic to you?" the results probably would have been different.

Also be on the lookout for the Ping-Pong effect. Sometimes you can spot it very early. You ask a question and everybody's head turns to you. Then when someone answers, the heads go to her. Somebody else talks and heads swivel again. I hate when that happens. It's too precise, too studied. I want to sit back and watch. If I open up my mouth, I want to be a participant who's looking for more information, not an interviewer who's asking another question. To stop Ping-Pong behavior, stand up, walk around, gesticulate, do anything to get people to talk to each other. You want the conversation to be more akin to that dinner-table chatter.

Your hands are as important as your mouth. Particularly when dealing with questions of percentages, degrees, spectrums, size, quantity, I prefer not to offer up numbers or specifics. I'll hold out my arms like a balance scale or use them to form the size of a package. Nonverbal cues put the onus back on panelists to fill in the blanks without imposing the moderator's expectations.

The first time someone mentions their brand, clients get anxious and want the moderator to hone in on the target. But you lose too much by doing that. It's very hard to respect a long pause when you've asked some question of a group and there's silence. But if you let it happen, somebody will volunteer.

Leave things hanging. A panelist may utter the magic words you've been waiting to hear but if you pounce on it, everyone in the room will be clued in. So store it for later retrieval. It's an artillery strategy: First fire long by almost ignoring the comment, then fire short by talking to someone else about a related subject, then zero in. By not letting the panel know that's what you're interested in, you get more valid answers.

I was conducting groups for Nyquil when Richardson-Vicks, the parent company at that time, was interested in coming out with an alcohol-free version of its popular cold medicine. They wanted to gauge consumer awareness and attitude toward alcohol in medications out of concern about what would happen if they removed it from the formula. They would have been quite content to have me ask, "What would you think if they took the alcohol out of Nyquil?" and lead users into a pointed and detailed discussion for an hour. But I wasn't sure people even knew that cold medications contain alcohol. We needed to probe how they felt about it without bringing up the word "alcohol" or tipoffs like drowsiness or grogginess.

We circled the topic with general conversation about treating colds, what they take and what Nyquil does. Finally, someone noted Nyquil's intoxicating effect, saying it was as if "I've had a Rusty Nail." Bingo. I let a couple of other panelists speak and went back to follow up. "Oh, Janice, you said Nyquil really took care of your cold symptoms and Mike, you said it worked but you hated the taste. Henry, you mentioned it was like, comparable to uh . . ."

The client might have thought I was an idiot. "Didn't she hear him. He said 'a Rusty Nail.'" But hemming and hawing made Henry feel very important. He listened to what I said, because when someone goes "uh, uh, uh," people want to help. He was going to make sure I understood. Once the subject was broached, it opened up the floodgates of discussion. If there's an inherent problem with a product, a brand, a premise, or a concept, panelists will eventually get around to it in their own words, and in their own time. In this case, I was able to tell the client that Nyquil users suspect that something in Nyquil makes them drowsy and groggy, and that the effects may be comparable to imbibing, down to experiencing a hangover the next morning. But, I didn't get the feeling that alcohol content was being isolated as the culprit. In fact, when we got around to it, a "nonalcohol formula" (later to become Dayquil) met with an enthusiastic response because they could take something to feel better during the day, and still know that what they took at night would "knock them out for the count." In this regard, alcohol-like effects were a meaningful reference point, but the ingredient alcohol seemed invisible to the consumer.

The best clients patiently let the group reveal its thoughts in this fashion. Those that want everything at the same point in every group, that require me to go around the table a lot, get uncomfortable very quickly. If they want the first 10 minutes always devoted to this and the next 15 to that, we're in trouble.

Creative Techniques

People laughed at Barbara Walters for her infamous question to Katharine Hepburn about what kind of tree she would be, but projected imagery can be extremely effective. With the profusion of similar products, brands have to differentiate themselves by carving their names in the consumer's mind. Projective work lets marketers take full measure of a brand's impact, to understand consumers' true feelings about services and products. Asking consumers to compare brands with trees, flowers, celebrities, TV shows, cars—whatever makes sense in their universe—gives them a way to express the characteristics of products in a new frame of reference. The other bonus: It keeps clients whose interest tends to flag, listening behind that one-way mirror.

Long before its most recent and successful reincarnation, I was doing a study for Tang with women who loved, adored, and used the brand regularly. It had great associations with the space program, their kids were crazy about it, and it was loaded with vitamin C. I asked panelists to imagine Tang as a person. Similar images kept recurring. Interestingly, no one saw Tang as an astronaut; Tang was somebody wearing a big orange cape that hid his face from his nose down so only his eyes were uncovered. We would get comments like, "I don't know why I have him hiding in this orange cape." In their heart of hearts, they knew Tang was artificial, a fraud, not real orange juice, but it was okay. It was a potent image that told us precisely what women thought about the brand.

Using automobiles as a suggestive technique works well, especially on the West Coast, where everyone is emotionally invested in their car. In California, projective car exercises result in esoteric comparisons that include the exact shape of the bumper and how it wraps round the front of the car. In New York City, where taxis, buses, and subways reign, cars draw a blank. If you're doing an interview with a person who's a cook, ask the person to give you examples from the food world. If someone's in real estate, ask for neighborhoods. Most of America uses television as a reference point. Try authors with English teachers. In our groups we've done odes, used tarot cards, written obituaries, and even used planets with hair dressers—anything just to get consumers to focus on products and brands from a different and often more revealing perspective.

The Truth and Focus Groups

Often, articles on focus groups imply that panelists may be dishonest. Well, I don't think people in focus groups lie on purpose. They fabricate answers because they don't understand the question or think they've said it already or don't want to embarrass you because they don't like the product. The lies reflect discomfort more than deliberate deceit. People get tangled up in their underwear when they lose track of where they're going and the point they want to make. Sometimes after you've asked a question every which way, you may get a note from the client saying, could you ask it this way? So panelists come up with a new way to answer. To give participants every opportunity to tell the truth, make sure there is nothing scary, threatening, intimidating, or confusing about the discussion.

Dealing with Difficult Panelists

People who need to be the center of attention can pose a big problem. Several years ago, I was working on a complex project for an American Express financial service. We were attempting to isolate the right potential positioning for the service and making little headway. We must have done 25 groups. Finally, we were out in Los Angeles, and at last we were getting it. We were really getting it. The written concept we were running past panelists now dragged on for three pages of copy, but at least people understood what we were trying to say.

The final group came in and there were three comedians who totally wasted our time. As much experience as I have with controlling people, I was down for the count against three LA comics. Every word in the concept drew a one-liner. They were doing monologues, they were writing sitcoms, they were rehearsing their stand-up act. It was horrible, and frankly, while it might have been all right to excuse one Seinfeld wannabe, putting the hook to all three would have been even more disastrous to the group dynamic. I appealed to their sense of fair play by bringing up the specter of audience hecklers. The reminder about dealing with a tough crowd jolted them back into being naive investors rather than sharp-tongued wise guys.

You can usually spot the class clowns in a group because they try to do something amusing before they even sit down. If you respond, you're trapped and headed for more. You can try to be clever and nice, but sometimes the only alternative is to turn your back and totally ignore them. Also, the rest of the group will help you because they don't like them any more than you do. They're just sort of a pain in the neck to everybody.

If you need a group of eight and nine people show up, and one woman has been pacing in the waiting area, looking at her watch whining about when are you going to start, you don't want her in your group. Or the guy who has been holding court—it's better to proceed without him. In facilities I use frequently, I ask whoever is checking in the panelists to warn me ahead of time about anybody who is a smart aleck, who uses off-color language, or who reeks of attitude. It's easier to eliminate them than to spend half of the limited discussion time playing schoolmarm.

A lot of the bad rap that focus groups sometimes get can be blamed on moderators' failings. The moderator must be able to cope with a range of personality types while firmly but unobtrusively directing the discussion. The loudest mouth shouldn't dominate, and the experienced moderator should be able to draw out the feelings of each panelist in relation to what others are saying.

Most professional moderators have developed an arsenal of invisible artillery to control extraordinary panelists. Observers watching the group conclude, "that was a good group of panelists. The moderator had an easy time of it."

If it looks this easy from behind the one-way mirror, this means that your moderator is doing a terrific job of controlling the group. If there's a loudmouth who's dominating the group, it's up to the moderator to reel her in and keep the other panelists' attention focused. The moderator should not be expected to dismiss the recalcitrant participant because the vacant seat will be even more upsetting to the group dynamic. Give the moderator time to deal with difficult panelists in her own manner and style, and you'll find panelists even more eager to cooperate and to talk about their private lives.

Straight Talk

I've done groups about incontinence, depression, osteoporosis, even baldness, and I've found the best way to deal with sensitive topics is head-on. Be forthright and get right to the point. Don't beat around the bush and come at it from different ways. People recruited for focus groups have already answered certain questions on the phone. They've agreed to participate knowing that they are going to be talking about something like this, so they've got enough guts to come in and you need to treat them with respect. I'll say, "Well as you know, we're all here to talk about incontinence. Is that everybody here?"

In groups, people bond with each other over a common problem that they're normally embarrassed to discuss. They form an ad hoc support group. In doing work on antidepressant drugs and depression in seniors, I found participants took great comfort in discovering that someone else has similar fears and concerns. If you're a little nervous about telling your grown daughter you're taking Prozac, it's a tremendous relief when another woman in your age group confides that she had the same anxiety.

LISTENING POINTS

- Listen and pay attention to everything—tonality, body language, seating, even silence.
- Lead the panelists to the subject without polluting the waters.
- Make the conversation informal and unstudied.
- Try nonverbal cues and unfinished sentences. Someone will jump in with an answer.
- Use your imagination to guide participants into using theirs.
- Create an atmosphere that encourages honest answers.
- Be prepared to cope with participants who seek the limelight.
- Deal with sensitive subjects sensitively but forthrightly.

5

TOTAL HEARING

The Art of Really Listening to Focus Groups

Yogi Berra once said: "You can observe a lot just by watching."
My spin on that is: "You can hear a lot by just listening."

Marketers use every icon, symbol, animal, sound bite, color scheme, mood, and attitude to attract consumers. Everybody wants to be listened to. Everybody has something important to say. Everybody has a product or service that is the greatest thing since the World Wide Web, if only consumers would listen. Marketers are like 3-year-olds, constantly pulling, tugging, wanting attention. So it is ironic that as much as they want the consumers to listen to them, marketers are often just too preoccupied to listen to their current, intended, or lost customers.

Did You Hear That?

Getting consumer feedback—whether it's from a next-door neighbor or panelists in a focus group—requires listening with an ear that translates what they're saying into what it means to your business. You have to listen hard and diligently to understand why they're interpreting your message the way they are. It's the only way you'll ultimately get on the consumers' wavelength.

Communication has significantly less to do with just being heard and a whole lot more to do with being understood. Only the consumer can tell you if your idea is comprehensible, meaningful, unique, and warranted. You may have written a great concept for a new product, all of your team may applaud it, legal may have signed off on it, and technical may have given you the green light. Focus groups test the waters for potential consumer response to an idea and how it's expressed. Listening to their feedback tells you what you're communicating.

In a project I did for Wishbone, one flavor they wanted to advertise in their new line of vinaigrettes was raspberry. Now *balsamic* may be part of your everyday conversation, but there are lots of salad lovers and bottled salad dressing users who aren't too sure what it is. Tell them a dressing is vinaigrette and their reaction is: "Oh, how awful, I hate the taste of vinegar." Aiming to impress on the consumer that their product would be a full-flavored vinaigrette, the agency creatives wanted feedback on what would be communicated when the raspberries were visually depicted as larger than life on the bottles. To our literal-minded bottled salad-dressing audience, this sounded absolutely dreadful. Their take: lots of vinegar poured into a bottle with lots of fruit juice.

In the dialogue between a company or product and the consumer, what the consumer takes away from that conversation may not always be what the advertiser intended. When meaning goes south, it's not necessarily because the message isn't getting through, but rather it's being interpreted in unanticipated ways. Focus groups help check the translation. Does the language work? Do the symbols make sense? Does the consumer make the implicit connection that the advertiser has in mind?

In further research for Wishbone, we learned that the company had developed a set of commercials with a surrealistic theme. They used Magritte-style visuals that had the tagline, "Taste's so real it's surreal." In them, you saw an artist with an easel painting a huge garlic on a canvas that itself bleeds into the scenery. It blends into the horizon behind the canvas where there's no garlic at all and it's a bottle of Wishbone vinaigrette in a vivid blue sky punctuated by big puffy cumulus clouds. One person in six groups said, "How clever: Magritte, and the clouds, surrealism, so real. Wishbone is really smart."

Typical for the rest were dialogues like: "What does surreal mean? It sounds like a made-up word. Is it in the dictionary?"

"Well what do you think it means?"

"It's so real it's better than real."

I'm thinking *okay no problem with surreal.* "What else do you get out of that?"

"It's got a lot of garlic taste."

"Why do you feel that way?"

"Well look at that big old garlic. It's right in that garlic press." (They mistook the easel for a garlic press.) "Tell me what else."

"It's probably very light tasting."

"How come?"

"Well, look at all those clouds. I'd be really worried that all that garlic and all the vinegar that must be in a vinaigrette would make the dressing strong and vinegary. Actually, I prefer ranch. But when I see all these clouds, it makes me think it might have a light taste."

In my view, the client couldn't ask for anything more. Despite their lack of familiarity with surrealism and its imagery, panelists got the message immediately. In fact, they were reading more into it than the advertising agency had even intended. So what if the easel wasn't a garlic press. Who cares that the clouds weren't meant to convey the idea of light tasting but were part of the Magritte mimicry. The client had a hard time believing it didn't matter that the results weren't intentional. Yet their inadvertent brilliance could lead to more purposeful advertising.

How do you sell more lemonade? Country Time lemonade's survey research indicated that most households didn't start stocking up on powdered beverages until May. A bright young marketer realized that if the consumer could be entreated to buy a month earlier, Country Time could push more of its "good old-fashioned lemonade." I was asked to pretest the new ads for Country Time to see if they could get that buy early message across.

The strategy for the first go-round of advertising featured various symbols, some as literal as a ticking clock, that reminded consumers how quickly summer passes. In no time at all, it's gone. The subtext for the spot was, *You better start drinking Country Time now to make the most of summer.*

The panelists heard the message but interpreted it not quite how the brand's execs had hoped. First, nobody wanted to be reminded how short summer was. It depressed them. Furthermore, they felt threatened, almost pressured, into stocking up before it was too late. One person described it as a "sky is falling" feeling.

Take two. Out went the clock. The next round of advertising emphasized the long, lazy, carefree days of summer. Lemonade and a languid July, backed by soothing jazz and a dulcet-toned announcer who draws us into the balmy experience. Doesn't it make you long for a cool drink?

Consumers warmly embraced the ads inferring that drinking Country Time lemonade extended that great summertime feeling. The company could start running those commercials in February.

Country Time was also testing commercials for its new Lemonade Iced Tea and developed a storyboard depicting a huge intergenerational family gathering, with grandparents at one table and younger people at another. Country Time was hoping viewers would catch the implicit message that iced tea brings families closer, ties them together. Instead, a majority of consumers remembered being stuck at the kids' table at family events, feeling left out and treated like second-class citizens. This emotional memory was so overpowering that no one even saw the giant pitcher of Country Time Lemonade Iced Tea on the table. They were mentally reviewing and emotionally reliving remembrances of being a powerless child. We only knew this because we asked panelists what they were thinking about when they saw the commercial—key learning we never would have obtained if we had asked: "What is the main point of this commercial?"

Checking References

When consumers think about your brand without prodding, what immediately comes to mind is a nugget of informational gold. Treasure it. The most unsullied perspective on the story is often the most valuable.

In focus groups, we try awfully hard to induce consumers to talk about a product as if they were in their natural habitat instead of our lab rat setting. If I'm researching Tic Tac and the client isn't sure whether to position it as a candy or a breath freshener, I'm going to lose that unaffected chatter if I introduce the topic as, "Today we're going to talk about breath fresheners. Please tell me how, when, where, and why you use breath fresheners." We'd wind up certain that Tic Tac is a breath freshener. If you begin without any assumptions—a white canvas—and introduce the topic in a totally clean environment, real learning takes place.

This is how a conversation might go:

Moderator: Today we're going to talk about things that you put in your mouth. I'm not really interested in chocolate. I'm more interested in minty kinds of things. Do you know what I mean?

First panelist: I always have some Tic Tacs in my purse, especially since I stopped smoking. I feel like I just want to put something in my mouth to kind of change the taste. And they taste good. And they're not fattening. What is it they say? They've got one and a half calories or something.

Moderator: When you say, "change the taste in your mouth," what does that mean? Are there other things that do that?

First panelist: Well those strong mints in a tin, those Altoids. Now they're really powerful. I'd rather put 5 Tic Tacs in my mouth than have one of those Altoids. With Tic Tac, it's more like just having something nice in your mouth. It changes the taste just enough. Like some mints are too much of a change and some don't do anything. Tic Tac is just enough.

Here's what I've learned and I'm hoping my client behind the mirror has heard. They're beginning hypotheses, little thoughts and possibilities that I stash in the back of my mind and listen for as other consumers continue to talk:

- Breath was never once mentioned. Maybe there's a way to position Tic Tac as a mouth thing to stand out from the breath freshener crowd.
- She's using them to replace cigarettes. Should we coventure with one of those stop-smoking patches?
- One and a half calories seems to be a supportive element for usage. Yet from the tonality in her voice, she's not too

certain about the claim. I know that it's important to my client, but if consumers are already aware of this, perhaps they don't have to spend a lot of time stressing it.

- Altoids don't seem to be a threat because they are stronger than what this Tic Tac user is looking for. And, isn't it interesting that she correlates five Tic Tacs with one Altoid.

- Finally, love the way she describes Tic Tac as "just enough." Wonder what we can do with that whole premise.

I was fishing for consumer feedback on new flavors that Maxwell House was considering for their brand of cappuccino mix. To set the tone, I started with, "Tell me about the hot beverages you drink." Going around the room, one woman volunteered, "What about that box of stuff?" and with gentle probing went on not only to describe the Maxwell House cappuccino product, but to acknowledge that sometimes she even preferred it to the cappuccino she bought at coffee shops.

What I heard was that while users might not seem to show respect for the product in discussing it, they like it. Nor is the maker fooling anybody in terms of what this mix is. The client was somewhat concerned, as most companies are when their brand is mentioned in less than glowing terms. Panelists had barely recognized Maxwell House cappuccino mix, relegating it to that stuff in the packet.

A bit more questioning and it became apparent that the users of that boxed stuff weren't out to make anyone believe that they had an espresso machine in the kitchen. They simply liked the mix for what it was—a good-tasting, change-of-pace hot beverage to have at home. No way did they ever feel it would compete with an on-premises Starbucks product.

Interestingly, the commercials that the agency had developed for the brand worked like a dream because they incorporated a wink at consumers to let them know that the company knows this isn't the same experience the user will have in a fancy restaurant after a delicious gourmet meal. The commercial had a couple in the kitchen using the mix and making obvious hissing sounds as they spooned the product into a cup of hot water. In another execution, an elderly user who is obviously trying to impress his lady friend emerges from the kitchen with the packet stuck on the heel of his shoe.

Put in context, the Maxwell House mix users know it's a convenience product; they know it's not brewed, they know it comes in a box—and the commercials reinforced that. The campaign's tonality and attitude were right on target and would go a long way to help consumers identify that box of stuff as Maxwell House.

In contrast, when I tested a set of introductory commercials for the brand, the agency had featured a group of Cappuccine friars quietly walking through the cloisters while a voice-over compared the Maxwell House product with the monks' brew.

Two things happened here that revealed how totally off the mark this approach was:

1. Packaged mix users had no idea what the connection was between the Friar Tuck-like characters and stuff in a box. No one knew the origins of cappuccino, and more importantly, no one cared.

2. The foam on the cup of cappuccino in the commercial was almost double the height of the foam that users actually got when they made the product at home. Buyers' advice to the listening client group, "Show the box foam, not the machine foam. Who do you think you're kidding?"

Mining for Meaning

People will tell you that they drink iced tea because it's refreshing. What does refreshing mean? How is iced tea refreshing different from lemonade refreshing or bottled water refreshing or carbonated beverage refreshing? Consumers will tell you about stains, but in Georgia, what they mean is red mud on their kids' clothes. In New Jersey, they're talking about iron stains from tap water. The mother with an infant has formula on everything, whereas the woman with the toddler describes apple juice in sippy cups as the enemy, and the parent with school-age child battles grass stains. You'll never find that out unless you refuse to accept information at face value.

Listening to consumers in a focus group is like shopping in a bazaar. Never accept the first price; never stop with the first answer. The answer is usually buried in the second, maybe the third response. There's a limit in bargaining, however, and if you go over the edge, the seller doesn't want to do business with you anymore. The same happens with asking questions. If you ask too many times, panelists begin to tell you falsehoods because it seems to them that you don't like their answers and you're looking for something else.

If a moderator stops probing at the first answer, you need another moderator. Put another way, it's like traveling in Third-World countries: You quickly learn that the question, "Do you have running water?" must always be followed up with, "Is it working?" and then "How often?" Don't assume that a response is necessarily an answer.

I was exploring the whole world of pretreatment laundry products, the stuff that comes in sprays or gel sticks or just in a big bottle that you can pour from. The market leader is Shout; my client was Spray 'n Wash:

Moderator: Let's talk about things you use when you're doing your laundry. Specifically, I'm interested in things you use in addition to detergents: things you may use when you see a stain or a spot or grease. Laura, let's start with you.

Laura: I love my Spray 'n Wash.

Moderator: You *love* it?

Laura: What I mean is that it works. Even stuff that's been through the dryer.

Moderator: Been through the dryer? What do you mean?

Laura: Well, if you've got a stain, you might miss it when you wash it, and then you put it in the dryer, the heat from the dryer really sets the stain. At that point, you're a goner. But I tried my Spray 'n Wash on it and it came out.

Moderator: So . . . ?

Laura: So, that Spray 'n Wash is really good stuff. Now some stains are just too tough even for Spray 'n Wash.

Moderator: Tough, like how . . . ?

Laura: Tough like impossible to get out because sometimes it's the fabric that you're dealing with that just grabs hold of the stain. Or sometimes I didn't get at it early enough. Like, the kids never tell you that they've messed up, and if you're not careful when you're loading, you can miss it. If it can be gotten out, Spray 'n Wash will do it.

My interpretation:

- "Love" is a powerful word to use for a pretreat. Emotional advertising will probably work here (more about emotional benefits in later chapters).
- Never ignore a comment like "it works." This means that the consumer is satisfied. The brand has broken out of the

realm of perceptual trust and entered the royal kingdom of absolute belief.

- Consumer proof of efficacy may be "the dryer test." Talk to technical to see if a compelling story can be made out of a claim like this.

- It's interesting that if stains don't come out, the pretreat user is more likely to blame another source. It's the fabric. It's the kids. It's the circumstance. It's me; I was too busy to notice it.

- Finally, what a great tag line for creatives at the agency to fool around with: "If it can be gotten out, Spray 'n Wash will do it."

When French's wanted to dip into the gourmet premium mustard business, they gave me a concept board to show focus groups. The board announced a great new French's mustard and briefly described the product, but there was no picture. At the bottom of the board, it said "4.5 ounce jars available for $2.99." My job was to pass it by consumers to see if they understood the product description prior to putting it into a large-scale survey and ascertain what aspect of the new mustard should be stressed as well as whether this familiar family brand could support a gourmet mustard price tag.

Panelists looked it over and generally agreed that it seemed like a wonderful mustard and the price presented no obstacle. Back behind the mirror, I could feel the contented glow of French's executives. A tiny alarm went off in my head. This seemed an expensive mustard for this audience. I couldn't believe that these 10 women, all of whom bought French's mustard because their children liked to slather it on sandwiches, were going to spend $2.99 for a small jar of mustard the kids could demolish in one lunchtime.

I instructed the group to "show me with your hands the size of the jar of mustard you are visualizing." And they all replied, "You know, the regular size jar" and indicated with their hands the familiar eight-ounce size. I went back to my clients, who were all chattering to each other. This wasn't the size they had in mind. French's revisited their mustard plans and rightly decided to stick with their family taste and family size product. Without further prodding, the "would buy" survey scores could have been off the charts, and French's might have plunged ahead thinking they had landed another space in consumers' refrigerators.

Getting the Most from Metaphor and Analogy

The average consumer isn't spending 24/7 exploring his latent antipathy toward building wrap, alcohol swabs, or oven cleaner (yes, I've done research on all of these), so focus groups rely on fanciful imagery and analogy to get panelists to see brands in a different light. However silly they may seem on the surface, they allow you to get further and further away from the tangible aspects of a product and get closer and closer to the emotional bond the consumer must feel with a brand.

I like to use simple metaphors. Imagine different brands as automobiles, neighborhoods, magazines, countries. Imagine different brands as different people. And lately, I've had a lot of success with imagining brands as total planets with cultures, mores, idols, topography, inhabitants, dress codes, and values.

Tropicana was considering coming out with a refrigerated apple beverage to be sold in cartons like their orange juice. We used this imagining technique to understand feelings about apple juice versus apple cider. I asked panelists to put themselves on cider and juice planets and describe who and what they saw.

Apple cider drinkers saw Planet Cider as a healthy, robust environment, where the air had the fresh feel and scent of a crisp fall day. Country scenes filled with friends and family, fireplaces, and fruit-filled orchards beckoned. Autumn red predominated. When they were on Planet Juice, the world changed to too-bright pinks and blues. The whining of children and babies could be heard and snack food was always on the menu.

When I did the same exercise with apple juice users, Planet Cider was an environment of rotten apples and petrified cores with the stench of fermentation. The inhabitants were gnomelike creatures who loved to squish apples by stomping peels. On Planet Juice, their world changed to beautiful pastels. The cooing of babies could be heard intermittently with the gleeful sounds of contented elementary school children at recess. It was day-care paradise.

The exercise helped Tropicana understand the appeal of cider as a serious, grown-up drink and differentiate between the juice- and cider-drinking audience. This was crucial information because the client had entered into the project under the assumption that apple cider would be perceived as a more natural, healthier, and a premium form of apple juice. They knew from orange juice drinkers that the closer to the orange and the further from the concentrate, the more premium the product. The same ipso facto formula didn't work with apples.

I also like to create a community because all the brands in any given category are really like a cast of characters, each with a certain personality right out of central casting. While panelists sometimes balk at this, you have to remind them that you are talking about gross generalizations and stereotyping, just as scriptwriters use on soap operas, and encourage them to bring out their whole arsenal of biases.

Yardley, a toiletries brand popular in the 1960s and 1970s, was trying to establish a positioning for itself after Maybelline had purchased it. The brand was going to be sold in drugstores, and the cosmetics giant was hoping it meant something to women in the 1990s.

We put out an array of brands that were competitive to Yardley—more downscale, more upscale, or interchangeable—and instructed panelists to imagine they were in a small town and to pick which brand would be the mayor, which the judge, which the police chief, and so on. Yardley was everything from the Lolita-esque adolescent to the dogcatcher to the elderly spinster librarian: The brand was in the midst of a prolonged identity crisis.

After the advent of Altoids on the breath mint scene, virtually all other brands in this category became has-beens, especially if they weren't advertising. When we asked panelists to construct soap operas using breath mints, invariably my client Tic Tac would come up as the extraneous character. It was always one of the nurses hanging out around the nurses' station in ER. Tic Tac was not the stalwart, hard-working, but somewhat quirky Hathaway; just one of several characters there to enhance the existence of the primary characters. The Tic Tac character never had a name. This didn't surprise me. Tic Tac hadn't been advertising for awhile, and without advertising, you become nameless. You don't get attached to people—or products—without names.

Silence Is Golden

As a moderator, when you feel as if you're eavesdropping in on a conversation, you know you're on the right track. I call it *learning to listen to answers that have no questions.*

Props are a great aid here because, when people handle products, the action replicates what goes on when they get to the shelf. I've done a couple of projects for La Prairie, an exclusive, premium-priced department store line of skin-care products. After showing women some prospective advertising, I took out some La Prairie products and placed them on the conference room table without saying a word. The women picked up the bottles, oohed and aahed, and marveled at the beautiful packaging. "Oh, this is that moisturizer in the ad. I see, this is really worth the price. It didn't look like this at all." Just this little exchange gave the client more than she bargained for. It hammered home the importance of the package in a campaign designed with the product as hero. The ad needed just a picture of the luxe bottle, not even a line of explanatory copy until the reader turned the page. It also supported the client's preexisting design judgment that the package wasn't being displayed to its best advantage. I didn't have to ask the tedious, "To what extent do you feel that this package looks like what's advertised?"

Product sorts—where we put out all the competing brands and ask panelists to organize them however they want—provide similar learning. I don't care which products are in which group. I'm interested in how they talk about the product when they pick it up, how they refer to it, and what title they give the grouping.

Sometime in the mid-1990s, Wise Foods introduced a line of low-fat salty snacks under the sub-brand, Wise Choice. Because sales had been disappointing, the company decided to identify strategies that might revitalize the line and to develop cohesive packaging. Often as brands are iterated over time and sub-brands beget sub-brands, with each successive brand manager seeking to put his or her own imprimatur on the product, the packaging gets messy, thereby confusing the shopper. When consumers are baffled, they flee.

Wise was interested in finding out what message their packaging should be communicating to consumers. To start with a clean slate, we didn't even show the Wise Choice packaging to consumers. Instead, we put together a couple of groups and just threw a batch of various bags of snacks down on the table and instructed panelists to sort them anyway that made sense to them. From our perspective, the only thing that all the bags had in common was that they were all salty snacks.

Consumers arranged the bags on a theoretical health scale, from super junk to the fat-free stuff that most panelists describe with words like "cardboard" and "tasteless," to the pretzel-like snacks that took all other salty snacks to task. But in between these worlds was a world of confusion for consumers. Each group had a different take on which brands and products went where, based on the mixed signals that the manufacturers were sending out. Product appearance seemed to say one thing, but the brand name promised something else. Often it was coupled with an ingredient list that increased cholesterol levels just from reading it, contradicted by starbursts of claims like "fat-free" or "baked goodness" that belied everything else.

Again, I didn't care which snacks went into which category; I cared about the consumer reasoning. My theory was that buyers couldn't immediately tell whether it was no-fat, low-fat, salty, healthy, or fattening. As panelists picked up bags of salty snacks and talked about them, their words bespoke consumer bewilderment, bother, and brand confusion created by product proliferation for proliferation's sake. Guaranteed, the thought process will be the same when shoppers arrive at the snack food display.

For example, Multi-Grain Sun Chips had just been introduced and was apparently taking the market by storm. Its packaging promised "30% reduced fat." Not surprisingly, some panelists put this bag in a reduced fat category since this was the product's main claim. It sounded reasonably healthy, was presumably made with whole grains, and might be somewhat lower in fat. Others argued that the chips belonged with the "super junk" on the experiential basis of having eaten them and then having read the ingredient label to find out that they were still relatively high in fat, salt, and calories, despite the deceptively healthy-sounding name.

I didn't have to put Wise Choice in the mix to conclude that however they designed their package, and whatever they claimed, the ingredient list should match the starburst claims. State your benefits—if it's healthier because it's baked, say it—and don't lose sight of product appearance as another conveyor of benefits. Most importantly, don't try to fool the consumer. In most cases, she's way ahead of you.

And the question I asked? Well, there wasn't one. The instruction to the focus group panelists: "Just do it." The instruction to the client behind the mirror: "Just watch and listen."

Reaching Out

Consumers will almost always tell you how best to reach them if you listen to their cues rather than the echo of your own voice. Assuming you understand their needs without hearing it from their mouths is usually a foolhardy endeavor.

Memorial Sloan-Kettering Cancer Center called me in to help them understand how best to advertise their stop smoking/wellness program. They thought if they emphasized how evil smoking was, people would see themselves in that negative portrait and realize they had to quit. They developed print ads showing a scene in front of a typical big city office building. Huddled outside in the pouring rain were the miserable smokers. Breezing through the doors, clicking his heels, was the happy-go-lucky guy who had quit smoking.

We put together groups with likely candidates for the program and showed them the campaign. The ads all backfired. People who want to stop smoking don't consider themselves as one step from hell. They detested the cheery nonsmoker. They identified with the huddled masses furtively dragging on their cigarettes. Instead of thinking that the program sounded promising and beneficial, they were longing to have a cigarette, and angry at being reminded that they were no more than second-class citizens as long as they smoked. Memorial Sloan-Kettering changed the focus of the campaign.

Before Vaseline Intensive Care came out with their successful line of sun-care products, they did focus groups with a range of people, including very fair-skinned types, to understand the dynamics of sun protection. As a person who tans easily and loves the sun, I assumed that the basic need of people with light complexions was to protect themselves from the sun and not get burned. That only scratched the surface; their hatred of the sun and the products available was palpable.

They talked about how sitting in the sun made them feel as if they were being scorched inside and out by a burning poker. They were desperate for shade, for cranked-up air conditioning. When this fair-skinned group applied their super 30 SPF, heavy-duty, sticky sunblocks, the sense of suffocation was even worse. Their fears had far less to do with burning and skin cancer than a loathing for the horrible internal discomfort caused by the sun. They craved sun protection that was light and refreshing, and would give them total comfort while being outdoors. The feeling they were after was of sitting under a long-limbed leafy tree, or the next best thing, a beach umbrella.

I looked around and every single pale-skinned panelist was shaking her head like a dashboard doll. They were all burning from the same sun wanting to be under the same umbrella. What a potent symbol to use on a whole separate line of products devoted to the sun sufferer. That's what I recommended to the executives at Vaseline Intensive Care. "Be the savior of the sun averse. *Every time you see our beach umbrella logo, you know it's a product especially for you.* You guys could own this category. Can't you hear the anguish in their voices, the pleas for help?"

They didn't hear them. Years later, I got a call from Maybelline saying they had just bought a French product called "Ombrelle" a sun-care line with a simple beach umbrella as its symbol. *C'est la vie.*

A similar situation occurred in work I did for Colgate as they were about to introduce a shampoo line into Malaysia. We conducted groups in the United States to lay the groundwork for the research they would do abroad. When we spoke to thin-haired women, I heard this yearning for products that would give their hair follicles a dose of Viagra. You could sense the lack of self-esteem directly related to straight, stringy hair. They didn't want to wear pageboys their entire life; they resented having to color their hair for body. If Colgate could come out with a line, say Finally for Fine Hair, this segment of women would bronze the bottles.

The self-defined fine-haired panelists weren't declaring, "I want a whole line of thin hair products." Focus groups allow consumers to express how they feel. Reading into how they were expressing those feelings, it was terrifically clear that a huge opportunity existed for Colgate. I'll bet that American women with thin, flyaway hair would have embraced a manufacturer who offered them a real choice. For Colgate, with a presence linked to toothpaste and dishwashing liquid, it represented too big a leap.

The hair-care industry is still missing out on this one. As I browse the Kmart and Eckerd shelves, I notice that while manufacturers continue to come out with new hair-care brands that have an array of different formulations, attempting to be all things to all people, none is focusing on selling a lot of product to one person.

In my experience, once a consumer finds a brand that is speaking directly to her, that brand becomes part of her DNA. That person will believe in the power of the brand so much that she will keep buying and stop looking.

Intention and Meaning

It's not enough that a commercial is well regarded, liked, and possibly memorable. If panelists don't seem to be agreeing with their intent, advertisers and marketers are ready to lunge for the panic button. Even though you don't hear exactly what you want to hear about your commercial, if it's creating a good feeling for your brand, take it and run.

Raisin bran is in a category like the *Today* show and *Good Morning America*. There's Post Raisin Bran and there's Kellogg's Raisin Bran. Sometimes one does better and sometimes the other. They just go back and forth, back and forth. Essentially, they're pretty much the same. In 1991, Post Raisin Bran was mounting a campaign to differentiate itself and give consumers a reason to buy Post. They decided they would position themselves as the premium brand.

They developed a commercial with a pleasantly plump dad. He wore glasses, his hair was a little messed up, a real guy. He was sitting with his young son at a breakfast table. The table was a little messy, no pitcher of orange juice and a glass on a tray with one perfect flower. He and his son were bonding. The dialogue went something like . . .

Dad: Wow son, isn't this Raisin Bran delicious?
Son: Look at how big the flakes are, Dad.

Dad: Yes, and see how plump and fat the raisins are.

Son: Gee, Mom sure knows what we like.

Dad: Yeah. I guess somebody loves you.

Along with it, they tested another ad that used a spokeswoman talking to the camera about what makes Post Raisin Bran premium. Its raisins are plumper; its flakes are bigger. Buy it, use it, very straightforward.

After seeing the first commercial, panelists allowed that Post Raisin Bran was "special" but they didn't play back the word, "premium." If Post Raisin Bran wanted to be thought of as premium, the talking head commercial was far more effective. It did considerably better in communicating that singular concept. Plus, the panelists voiced a few negatives about the Somebody Loves You ad. A few objected to the line about mom. They thought it was condescending for the two characters to be sitting at breakfast talking about how mom cares about me. Nothing scares clients faster than the possibility of creating negative feelings about the family unit.

However, the father/son commercial had several interesting aspects. First, it had generated much more conversation. Often what consumers tell you as they explain why they don't like something, will alleviate misgivings. Unless it's totally objectionable, when consumers say "I don't think that would happen in real life," it means they're going to watch it. They're getting the point and the whole plot line very quickly.

Second, people responded to seeing a regular guy who wasn't the usual boob of a father. Commercials like to cast wife/mother as hero and father/husband as nitwit. By playing up a somewhat realistic, warm father-son relationship, the ad succeeded in generating an emotional tug.

Clients think the consumer is literal (they are), but marketers take the gold medal. Rather than listening intently to four individual groups of consumers who indirectly were telling them that the father/son execution had a lot of stuff going for it, they wanted to see figures showing that the word "premium" was mentioned by 55 percent of those who saw the ad. They wanted "premium" not "special."

We probed deeper about what special meant: healthy, a great morning starter, good taste, and a cereal that parents as well as children like. Special seemed pretty good. It would be pointless to go back and rework the whole commercial and say premium eight times. They had a commercial that was far more likely to stick in consumers' minds, created an overall positive feeling for the brand, and communicated how "special" it was. Despite the initial misgivings, Post dropped the premium positioning and followed through with Somebody Loves You.

Tangential Information

When panelists talk about everything other than what's in front of them, they hate what's in front of them. Consumers don't really want to say bad things; they're trying to be helpful, so if they get lost on a tangent, something is wrong.

Starbucks was planning its assault on supermarkets and one of their advertising agencies had come up with print ads they hoped would let shoppers know that now they could buy their coffee beans in their local supermarket. Panelists saw the proposed campaign and changed the subject. They got into a discussion about how when they take Starbucks home, it just doesn't taste the same. Is it the water, the beans, the coffeemaker? They kept trying to evade the subject.

I got a note from the client—*Bonnie, get them back on track.* But the reason they were off track is that the ads made absolutely no sense to consumers. One had a cowboy mug, so panelists figured the brand being advertised was Cowboy Coffee. There was Starbucks@home, which only in the marketers' minds meant, *Now you can buy Starbucks at the supermarket where you live and bring it home.* To consumers, it suggested that they could get Starbucks online, since "@" has become a definitive Internet icon.

Another ad with red circles totally confused the panel into thinking that it might be a Target stores advertisement. Hence their conclusion: Starbucks is now available at Target. Sorry Starbucks, the red circles are owned by another brand.

All the scattered Starbucks iconography drew more blank looks. The only thing that registered was a little supermarket cart hidden away in a corner. The client shot the messenger—me— and hired a new moderator, who came up with the exact same findings. Today, when you see the ads for Starbucks in supermarkets, the one thing that remains from our tests is the shopping cart.

Sensitivity Training

In con games, the object of the ruse is variously called the mark, the pigeon, the patsy, as a way of dehumanizing and distancing the cheater from the guy being duped. Guerrilla marketing tactics generate a similar mentality. A by-product of the "us versus them" mind-set is the inability to listen with the kind of heartfelt understanding that will help convert what you hear into products, services, and marketing efforts that resonate. Once you start to view the customer as a colleague and collaborator, rather than as a mark to be conned, you're in a better position to form a lasting and meaningful relationship.

People will talk honestly and say more to someone who listens with compassion even if the listener doesn't share their problem. I don't have to be incontinent to be compassionate with people who are. By empathizing with consumers, you're more apt to discover how best to address their needs. In hearing women over 50 talk about osteoporosis for Novartis, we had to counteract the indifference many women experience when they talk to their doctors in rushed conversations about menopause and osteoporosis. In having women discuss issues and misconceptions, we learned that the fear of loss of independence provided the best motivation to seek information and, if necessary, treatment. A company that forthrightly addressed the causes, myths, and impact of osteoporosis in a campaign that saw older women as vital and productive, not as hunched over with a dowager's hump, would gain their acceptance.

Listening from Start to Finish

Marketers need to listen to everything that's said. My experience is that clients lean forward and press their noses against the backside of the one-way mirror when I say to the panelists, "Now I'd like to show you some ideas." That's when they begin taking serious notes. What happens before then, though, may actually determine whether the idea that seemed so brilliant on paper has a chance to survive in the marketplace. Listening from start to finish provides the necessary context to judge the validity of panelists' response.

Just as Rodin knew what to take away from a chunk of marble, you need to be able to recognize a good idea lurking in the midst of conversational clutter. Offhand comments and asides that may have nothing to do with the main research frequently provide the most fruitful information. If one person says it, that's moderately interesting. When a chorus repeats it, that's a pattern. Pay attention, even if it isn't what you expected to hear.

Some time in the 1980s, the makers of Excedrin, a painkiller whose primary ingredient was aspirin, asked me to test consumer reaction to labels for new products. Typically, brands that are struggling to hold their own in a cluttered market fight back by coming out with their own version of what's killing them. In this case, Excedrin was losing ground to new over-the-counter remedies. So the company decided to put out its answer to Tylenol (an acetaminophen, even though no one knew what that was) and Advil (an ibuprofen, and no one knew what that was either).

The purpose of the study was merely to see whether they should use a label that said *Excedrin Ibuprofen* or one that said *Ibuprofen from the makers of Excedrin.* I set up appropriate groups with people who used analgesics. We showed everybody all the labels. Although there wasn't exactly rampant enthusiasm over drug-bottle labels, another message came in loud and clear from panelists: "Excedrin. Gee, I haven't thought about Excedrin for years. It worked great for headaches." And, "When I was hung over, and my head was pounding, I always took Excedrin."

There were six groups, and Excedrin and headaches correlated in every session. It was also likely that Excedrin could come out with either ibuprofen or acetaminophen, and the package designers learned enough about how their designs communicated to know the next steps to take in the labeling effort. The real opportunity resided in the brand's remarkable equity in headaches. The advertising simply needed to emphasize *Excedrin is the tough headache medicine.*

I reported my findings on labels to the Excedrin executives, and as I finished the presentation, casually mentioned the panelists' strong connection between the brand and headaches. Eyes brightened, heads nodded. As it turns out, that was an advertising positioning under consideration. One less headache for Excedrin . . . consumers already accepted that the product would bring them relief.

In another project for French's mustard, we were investigating several commercial possibilities to see which one best communicated that their mustard represented fun, a product the whole family used and enjoyed. Their agency made up a few storyboards and threw in some music to make the commercials seem more realistic. The consumers I interviewed had no problem getting the spots' main points. But what I reported to the client and ad agency was that people's faces absolutely lit up when they heard this toss-away jingle "Smile, You've Got French's." They had struck pay dirt with five notes. French's had never intended the refrain to serve heavier duty than as background for the test, but they listened and recognized that they had inadvertently stumbled on a winner. The song became the staple of the whole brand's ad campaign.

Counterbalancing

When you've done your best to be objective and independent, then you put your own reality template over consumer comments. When a research and development guy from Nabisco, new on the job and new to American marketing, heard kids explain in great detail how they ate Oreos by separating the wafers and eating the cream center and each wafer individually, he went back and developed a cookie that no child could rend asunder (Nabisco nixed the Oreo reinvention).

You weigh supposed interest with what you know about how consumers actually behave. Research shows that Americans talk lean but often buy fat. They claim to want dry, dry, dry wine but the reality is their taste runs to sweet. It's a counterbalancing act. You listen hard, then take the ideas out of the microcosm of the focus group and apply real-world standards.

When the late lamented Air Wick brand decided that air fresheners for closets was a real consumer need, we did a couple of focus groups on some wonderful designs and delivery systems that hung from hangers, were what the hanger was made of, and could be tucked into sleeves and pant legs. Bottom line: Yes, fresh-smelling closets is a real consumer need, but she's got a potpourri of products (including potpourri) already at her disposal; in the end, she's unlikely to purchase a specific closet refresher.

Counterbalance. Think about possible product success or failure from the consumer's point of view, long term. What the consumer wants and needs remains only half the picture. Focus groups help you make your own decisions if you are willing and able to run the data through your own reality screens.

Listening for Why

In defense of focus groups, I often point to an experience when I was doing work on fragrances for Prince Matchiabelli, a brand of the 1960s and 1970s, formerly owned by Chesebrough-Ponds, and now, quite possibly and deservedly defunct. People who make fragrances are always trying to identify the next hot scent because a perfume is just a brand name with an image. Once they have that, then they go out, develop the eau d'whatever and put it in a bottle that costs far more than its contents. The head of the brand had a theory that perfumes were all about sex and that's how he wanted to position their scent of the moment. We did group after group, interview after interview and none bore out his assertion. Wearing perfume was vaguely related to magnetism and luring the opposite sex, but really had much more to do with the scent's appeal to the woman herself. No woman would wear a fragrance that she didn't like just because it was going to attract somebody else.

The executive challenged the findings: "I know there's got to be a way to get deeper into a woman's sexual psyche about fragrance, I know it." One of his underlings suggested they get a hypnotist. They hired one. He spoke about fragrances to women under hypnosis and got them to go back, back, back into their deepest aroma motivations. The results were exactly the same as the ones reached in focus groups.

In the not-so-distant past, marketing researchers desperate for information about consumer response to advertising resorted to psychogalvanometers (contraptions akin to lie detectors that measure sweat and saliva). They also have used *Tachitiscopes*, or T-scopes, little devices that measure eye blinks, to gauge the drawing power of packaging. And there is an electronic instrument that tells you when a viewer's attention starts to wane while watching a commercial so that advertisers know where to introduce the brand name.

Today, the moisture meters have been scrapped (I'm not sure they ever pointed the way to a successful advertising strategy); they're probably still T-scoping; and new technologies come out daily that promise to predict consumer response. Companies continue to fixate on uncovering the ways brands resonate with buyers—when they do, when they don't, and how often.

Supermarket bar codes and computer cookies now track shopping and buying patterns. Soon, technology that allows us to click on our TV screen to order the product being advertised will also tell the manufacturer who we are. These high-tech approaches will identify who, where, when, and what. But they will never tell you why. However high-tech these solutions become, they cannot plumb the subconscious attitudes and desires that underlie behavior. And understanding why is what ultimately determines successful marketing.

There's a tendency to dismiss focus groups and face-to-face consumer research because consumers may not tell the truth, or they have hidden agendas, or too much group bias goes on, or people can't express their innermost feelings. Conventional wisdom takes it one step further to suggest that only by eliminating the human factor can we ever be certain that we've understood human motivation. I'm not a Luddite, but I think it's important to use human communication to understand human motivation and your own innate logic to understand your customer's logic. The human psyche makes or breaks your best-laid marketing and business plans, time and again. It's where well-planned, well-conducted focus groups take you. They're only as good as your ability to employ your imagination and intuition, informed by experience and context, to dig past superficial responses in pursuit of feelings consumers rarely know they have.

Listening Points

◎ Consider how consumers are interpreting your message. They'll tell you what you're communicating.

◎ Without prodding, pay close attention to how someone mentions your product.

◎ Dig deeper and you will be rewarded with deeper truths.

◎ Employ creative techniques to jump-start thinking along different paths.

◎ Listen for the subtext. It will cue you into consumers' attitudes and what will appeal to them.

◎ Think highly of your customer. She is an essential player on your team.

◎ Modify findings to match your own reality template. There is no market for instant toast.

◎ Use face-to-face human communication to get to the heart of human motivation.

6

CONSUMER'S RULE

Seeing the Consumer's Perspective on Products

Consumers come prewired. They process decisions based on preexisting mindsets and agendas. They behave according to a commonsense plan—theirs not yours. If it looks like a duck and quacks like a duck, people are going to put it in a pond. If your bottle of Resolve Steam Cleaning liquid comes in a big red laundry-size container with a giant laundry-size measuring cap, guess what the consumer will think your product is meant for?

To develop a cogent marketing plan and identity—a brand strategy—the first step is taking a 360-degree look at who you are. Marketers need to recognize and ask fundamental questions about their brand from the consumer's perspective. Qualitative research allows you to hear and apply the voices of consumers at all stages of the process, from the glimmer of an idea for new products through development, from packaging to labeling, from ad concepts to full-tilt executions, from brand launches to brand extensions to brand resuscitations. How do they see, categorize, relate to, interact with your idea, your advertising, your product, and your brand? And while you're at it, how do they feel about your competition? In the end, plugging in the consumer component benefits both company and customer.

Okay, you have a bright idea. (Remember 90 percent will end up in the recycle bin.) Decisions informed by the valuable learning and insights gained through focus groups and consumer interviews can save creative as well as capital outlay. Most companies wouldn't dream of proceeding without research, yet with the need for instant gratification—speed to market, being first, squashing the competition, getting more space on the shelf—the customer can often become the one screw left out when assembly is required.

Consumer Files

Companies can confuse what they're offering with how the consumer views their product. Or they misread the reasons for their competition's success, thinking they can substitute imitation for innovation. Before you go waltzing off into the next iteration of your brilliant idea, check out your standing with your potential audience. It's easier to change a product or ad, than a mind.

For years, Woolite has been dying for customers to use their product in bulk in the gentle cycle of the washing machine, instead of pouring a measly capful in the bathroom sink. In the generations of women who have become outrageously loyal to Woolite, we may have been able to make the earth-shattering transition from Woolite powder to Woolite liquid, but it has passed down as accepted wisdom from mother to daughter that we need use only a capful, whether we're rinsing one pair of pantyhose in a basin or a big load of pricey underwear and bras in the gentle cycle.

Luckily for Woolite, users had been satisfied with the results. Adding more of the product might increase the cleaning value, but Woolite users were more concerned with the special care they believed Woolite gave their "fine washables." Unluckily for Woolite, using tiny capful after tiny capful meant bottles sat around laundry rooms for years, the detergent equivalent of the car driven only on Sundays by the little old lady from Pasadena. In home ethnographic work we did, the client was aghast at the manufacturing dates she found on the bottoms of these small-capped plastic bottles.

Unable to change the consumer perception that you need only a thimble's worth for 1 item or 30, Woolite opted for another strategy. If you look in your local supermarket today, you'll find that large Woolite bottles *with huge caps* have nudged their way onto the same shelf as the big boys like Tide and All.

Companies sometimes undertake brand inquiries about the competition, hoping they can simply reproduce and rival the original. What they come to realize is that a brand is more than the sum of its ingredients, which makes copycatting a tenuous strategy.

Lysol had a pine-scented cleaner that was languishing on shelves, unable to make a dent in the market owned by Pine-Sol. The big Lysol idea: Come up with a new way to position itself vis-à-vis Pine-Sol. Thus, I was hired to investigate the power of Pine-Sol.

One of Pine-Sol's hallmark properties is that when you add it to water, it gets fizzy and hazy. It's called the blooming action (if you ever mixed water with the Greek liqueur ouzo, you've experienced a similar phenomenon). The research and development team was extremely anxious to know more about this blooming. They were certain it was a key factor in its popularity. Their theory was that users believed in the brand because this blooming property was almost magical; it transforms Pine-Sol before your very eyes.

In the midst of the first session, I began to get a stream of notes. *R&D wants to know more about the blooming action. What do they think about when they see the blooming action? Probe blooming.* Having listened to hundreds of women talk about every minute detail of cleaning and laundry, I was reasonably certain that unless it was going to bloom into a rose, this was a dead end. In all the groups for APCs (all-purpose cleaners), I had never once heard any Pine-Sol user comment on anything resembling bloom. It was all fragrance, the piney, woodsy smell.

Still, it was worth looking into blooming. We decided to get a bucket and pour some water and Pine-Sol in and see how the group reacted.

I returned to the panel room, bucket in hand, put in the water, and the Pine-Sol, and watched it bloom. The panelists all sat there and said, "Yeah, what are we supposed to do?" I said, "Well just look at it." They said, "Yeah." "Do you notice anything?" "No." "Well, it's . . . ," waiting for them to finish my sentence. Silence. "Look at how it's changed," I prompted. "Oh yeah." "Does it mean anything to you?" I queried further. "What do you mean? Mean what?"

It was absolutely worthless. What many Pine-Sol users, especially Latino ones, vividly recalled were childhood memories of that particular smell. Though it has begun to fade with greater assimilation, in the Hispanic culture the pine fragrance represented clean because grandma and great grandma used real pine oil to clean. The association was so strong that Pine-Sol had locked up this positive scent memory. Consumers weren't only purchasing a product, they were buying a piece of cultural history. What happened as the product and water were mixed together was meaningless compared to the potent memory of clean that the pine aroma evoked.

The Consumer Unleashed

To Clairol's absolute dismay, there are women who use hair coloring to dye their eyebrows, a practice that poses certain health risks. (The company apparently doesn't want to develop a safer product and own that particular market.) Makeup artists and models have known for a long time what the rest of the public is catching on to—the hemorrhoid-shrinking product Preparation H can be applied as a short-term solution for lines and wrinkles. And after years of Skin-So-Soft being used as an insect repellent, Avon finally gave in and started coming out with products that acknowledge that purpose.

The moral here is that we use products in ways that make perfect sense to us, if not to their manufacturer. Consumers often find unintended applications for goods. Listening to what happens once products leave the store can impact what new ones you develop, proscribe the limitations of your brand, or open up new avenues that can extend your reach.

What's great about focus groups is you realize all the assumptions consumers make that you never think about as a marketer. I did a study on smooth surface stoves. They're made from a glass ceramic, and in most cases when you buy them, the manufacturers give you a manual that warns not to clean the stovetop with glass cleaner because it will ruin the surface. Typically, the appliance store salesperson will say: "You have to buy this special paste. It only costs $9.99, and if you buy five at once I'll sell it to you for $40. But only use this cleaner on the stove top."

As consumers, we listen with half an ear. What we learned in talking to homeowners with glass surface stoves is that probably half are using Windex to clean the top. It is glass. Our intuitive logic is strong, something marketers have to keep in mind and that often pops up in focus groups. Why wouldn't I use a glass cleaner on a glass surface?

We infer how to use products from the signals manufacturers provide; we are conditioned to take cues from colors, type of bottle, iconography, and the goods that share space on a particular shelf. Pressed for time, we instantly process that the packaging on Product X looks like the packaging on Product Y and deduce that they're to be used in a similar fashion.

Consumers underscored that point for Resolve, an excellent carpet cleaner, and for years, the leading brand. As home-model, steam cleaners for carpets started cropping up about five or six years ago, Resolve came to me to research how customers who own or rent the cleaners would feel about putting Resolve in the machines rather than the products that come with the appliances.

We talked with consumers and found that most of these new steam-cleaner users didn't want to tamper with manufacturer instructions. "I bought Eureka and Eureka says 'use the Eureka product.' They have a tag on there that says if you use anything but the Eureka product, they're not responsible for any malfunctioning."

It's comparable to our anxiety about removing mattress tags. Going against the grain of such a strong conviction didn't make Resolve for home steam cleaners seem like a feasible idea. The appliances were so new to market that customers were reluctant to put in anything that could potentially gum up the works.

Nor was Resolve going to make inroads with anyone who rented the machine at a supermarket or home center. There was no way that renter was going to try a product other than what the manufacturer recommended. All that woman wanted to do was get that machine home and hope her husband hadn't gone out golfing so she could get those filthy carpets cleaned. She certainly didn't want to go back to that store and be told "this cleaner is clogged so we're not going to give you back your deposit."

Several years went by and Resolve wanted to reexamine the possibilities. The world has changed and there are many more steam cleaners around, and we're not so scared of them anymore. The positioning the marketing people came up with was terrific.

You don't use Maytag detergent in your Maytag washer. Why are you using a Eureka product in your Eureka steam carpet cleaner? Why not use Resolve. We know carpets because we're the leading carpet cleaner.

It was a compelling argument. Whenever you get the consumer's wheels turning and saying "that makes sense, I never thought about it like that," you're halfway home. On the other side of the mirror, they were tossing back M&Ms with abandon. Everybody was feeling great and it looked like we had something here. We showed the package, which was red like original Resolve, but everything else about it said Tide. It had a handle grip like detergent and a cup on the top like detergent. I told the group that this is what it would look like and everyone sighed.

"What's the matter?

"I would never know this was for my steam cleaner. I would just think Resolve is coming out with a laundry detergent."

Again, it was a perfectly logical conclusion. They had a great product and great positioning, but consumers weren't going to be able to distinguish it on the shelf. The other thing I intuited is that the marketers had probably never used a steam-cleaning machine. They thought the measuring cap would be a big selling point, as with laundry detergent. What they didn't realize—and what the consumer knows—is that the measuring cap is pointless because the user pours the cleaner directly up to a level line marked on the appliance.

Our programmed response coupled with an aversion to instructions often creates hurdles for new twists on familiar products. Everyone loved the concept of soy bacon but when Lean Strips was first tested, it failed miserably. All of the characteristics considered important for the new ersatz bacon received positive scores. People were high on its health benefits. It looked like bacon. It tasted like bacon. It was the same size, thickness, and color as bacon. However, sales were disappointing because consumers claimed it burned. Yet it didn't burn in the tech kitchen.

So we watched real consumers in a test kitchen. We gave them Lean Strips and instructed them to do exactly what they did at home. They emptied the slab into the pan, commenting that if they didn't know better, they'd think this was real bacon. "What," I asked "do you do next?"

"Well, usually I know how much time I have and so I go make the bed," came one reply. "When I hear the bacon sizzling, I know it's time to come back and separate it."

Another said: "I put the bacon up and then go empty the garbage."

"I prepare the pancake batter," explained a third woman.

Lean Strips looked so much like bacon that consumers treated it as if it were the real thing. No one stopped to read the carefully worded directions that indicated soy bacon cooks in considerably less time.

In probing how consumers interact with products, my goal is to take them away from a seat at the table and into standing in their kitchen, or sitting in their car or pushing a cart down an aisle. I want to observe people in their natural habitat, and save that, have participants re-create their behavior as closely as possible. When people describe what they do, they offer a glimpse into their lives. The more you understand how consumers go about the business of life, the more likely you are to be able to deliver meaningful messages and products.

I was involved in a Lysol project at the time of burgeoning anxiety about salmonella. Lysol had developed a commercial that showed an egg carton dropping and splattering on the floor. Our heroine picks up her bottle of Lysol Anti-Bacterial Kitchen Cleaner and a sponge to clean up this mess. And the panelists said almost in unison: "Uh, uh. Not the way it happens. I'm not going to spray until I get that stuff up with a paper towel. I wouldn't use a sponge on that. I would never just spray Lysol. There's shells in there."

Once again, perfect sense. Of course, you would wipe up the eggy mess before reaching for the spray and that's how the advertiser should show it. The same consumer would be groaning at the TV rather than hearing the brand message if the ad showed up in its original form.

I was hired to explore consumer behavior for Gevalia Coffee, a Swedish mail-order brand. They had built up a nice-size, loyal customer base by starting out with a come-on: *Buy a couple of pounds of Gevalia and we'll give you a free coffeemaker. If you don't like it, no commitment.* They lost a fair number of coffeepots, yet when Gevalia sent out letters noting a price hike, their drinkers kept filling the cup.

Gevalia was interested in what new materials they should put in the kit subscribers received with the coffee. The Gevalia executives correctly assumed that they had a special relationship with their customers. The company would send them a newsletter about the coffee plant, how great the coffee is with Swedish crumpets, new blends they could try. There were brochures on how beautiful Sweden was in the springtime, pictures of Stockholm harbor, and profiles of the brewmaster Ingmar.

In the sessions, I put the Gevalia carton down on the table. "Show me what you do when the coffee box arrives." Notice, no question was posed. I wanted to eavesdrop. They took the box, opened it up, took out all the materials, threw them aside, and dug down for the coffee. Nobody ever read anything that came in the kit. They would separate out any samples Gevalia put in the box. If the sample was glued on to anything written, they'd rip it off.

Consumers didn't know or care about this smorgasbord of tourist information. They couldn't even pronounce Gevalia but they liked it because it was excellent coffee, which was sufficient reason for customers to buy it. Gevalia's advertising today is totally focused on the product's appeal to discerning coffee drinkers. The Swedish connection is invisible.

Another interesting sidelight was that Gevalia customers were really attached to the box. All the nonsense inside didn't interest them at all. The box represented value. It was a sturdy cardboard box. And it said Gevalia, Gevalia, Gevalia, like the LV on Louis Vuitton bags.

As an anthropological field researcher, Margaret Mead was not content to sit up in ivied academe and merely wonder about coming of age in Samoa. In our arena, we have Linda Haviland, a keen observational researcher who has established a loyal following of clients who tag along as she takes them into consumers' homes for hours at a time, sometimes for an entire day, to watch how people use products and brands in their natural surroundings. Linda had been asked by a major vacuum cleaner brand to run one of her suburban safaris to observe how people vacuum.

The clients went into the project thinking suction ruled the day and had developed a superpowerful vacuum cleaner. They had tested it in a 9-by-12-foot flat unobstructed area, where they would put down a piece of carpeting and vacuum. It worked great. They ran it over shag rugs and low pile, synthetics and wools, old carpeting and new. The machine was fantastic as it continued to pass test after test.

Linda took the clients into real homes and suddenly they had an epiphany. Suction took a backseat to maneuverability. They saw women struggling up and down a staircase with the canister, trying to get it underneath the armoire and the sofa, going from wood to carpeted floors in an instant and catching rug fringe in the vacuum beater. Yes, the prototype sucked . . . a bit too much for the customer. The upside was that it gave the manufacturer new avenues to explore in creating a more practical model.

The eternal hope is that you'll do a focus group and the consumer will say something brilliant that will lead to something new: a new insight, a new product, a new way to think about a brand, a new usage phenomenon that will help you sell twice as much. It hardly ever happens. Not because consumers aren't doing their job but because businesses aren't watching and listening.

It happened with dishwashing liquid. Decades ago, researchers watched people at home use a bar of soap on the counter and a sloppy old sponge to wash dishes. They noticed that the consumer would take the soap and sponge and make a slurry, a gelatinous mix that resembled . . . liquid dishwashing detergent.

A little more lateral thinking and dishwashing liquid begat liquid soap. There is an abiding theory: New forms and new delivery systems will get me new sales and new customers.

Liquid soap, then, was a concept made in heaven. The groundwork had been laid in other cleaning categories, so why not in the shower and by the basin? I started testing these liquid soap concepts in the early 1970s. Consumers couldn't accept the new way to suds up because they couldn't wrap their hands around it. Everybody remained loyal to the bar. Men in particular liked the friction action of bar soap with the hair on their chest. They were convinced the viscous liquid wouldn't produce a lather. No matter how much we spoke about rejuvenation, that manly feeling, and germ-killing prowess, they couldn't get into it. Women were lukewarm about the idea too. They didn't know where they would put it. They didn't have room in their shower for another bottle. The kids would misuse it anyhow.

Despite that, someone finally broke through the liquid soap barrier. It wasn't any of my clients. It was a smaller player in

Minnetonka, Minnesota, who had the guts to pursue it. From watching and listening to consumers, he knew what would be the best place. His secret was to get out of the bathroom and back into the kitchen. He put liquid soap in a pump and placed it by the kitchen sink. Now, if your hands were greasy from making hamburgers, you could use your elbow to press down on the pump. Clean hands, clean bottle. People stopped reaching for their dishwashing liquid and began to pump their soap.

What this entrepreneur did was to step outside the product and see it from the consumers' perspective. All of the other manufacturers were trying to sell it as a soap replacement in the highest use area, the bathroom. He introduced it as a new product with its own benefits in the kitchen area. He hyped the pump and its convenience.

Companies often lack the patience to wait for consumer behavior to change and it's expensive to help that change come quicker. That leaves the territory ripe for the optimist who believes that he or she has the right product and understands where it fits in the consumer's lifestyle. I've seen products or ideas that I tested in one incarnation, finally come out 10 years later in another incarnation. Sometimes the consumer catches up with a trend; other times the manufacturer has timed market introduction perfectly.

The big packaged goods people only wanted to get into the bath and the shower because that's where their main business— bar soap—was. They all said, "It's not big enough," which is often the way big packaged goods people feel. This guy figured: A several million-dollar business—I'll take it. Not only did he come out with what everybody else was calling liquid soap, he trademarked the name *Softsoap.*

As people started using it, Softsoap began sneaking into the bathroom. Kids liked it for washing their hands. It did away with that ugly sliver of soap and dirty soap dish. Before long, there were decorator canisters and refills, leaving the big guys brainstorming in a boardroom trying to come up with products and names for what the consumer was generically calling soft soap. Procter & Gamble gave up trying and wound up buying the Softsoap company.

Products have to make sense in real people's lives. In trying to come up with healthy and convenient food, Stouffer's often heard women complain that though the pictures of fresh, green broccoli on Lean Cuisine packages were appealing, when they made the frozen dinner at home, the veggie turned into steamed gray mush.

After considerable pondering, we came up with the idea of putting the broccoli in a little steamer pouch. You would put the frozen entrée in the microwave and add the steamer pouch only for one minute. Then you would take out the broccoli and nuke the rest for another minute. That's how you would produce crunchy, emerald broccoli.

The double check: Ask consumers to imagine themselves using it in actual situations. "Get into your home, push the button of your microwave door, open it, tell me what's going on around you." That's when women visualized their 3-year-old spilling a bowl of his own lunch on the floor. Or they were at work and just wanted to scarf something down because they needed to rush out for a meeting, and the proposal wasn't quite finished.

After giving it some thought, the women had a different take. "It's adding another step. Then it's no longer convenient," they argued. Pale overcooked broccoli was a compromise the consumer was willing to make. In her mind, this wasn't ever going to be gourmet food. Fast, convenient, and reasonably healthy were sufficient. She'd live with the soggy vegetable.

Manufacturers are constantly trying to come up with a new wrinkle on an old product. When they listen to consumers, they often discover that they may already have what they're looking for.

The makers of Chore Boy, a brand of sponges, figured they should come out with a new sponge form to compete with a brand that had introduced one shaped like an hourglass, producing a spike in sales. The sponge's allure: easy to grasp. So Chore Boy sent its team off with a pair of scissors and they proceeded to cut off corners, nick the sponges in different places, and trim away to try any shape that might make a difference.

We passed the cut-up sponges around for consumers to hold and see how they felt in their hands. To steal the good grip thunder, the marketers had even created a version that resembled brass knuckles, thinking consumers would enter the store and say "I'm going to get that sponge, the one that's got finger indents" since who pays careful attention to brands of sponges?

Consumers were less than ecstatic. Typically, they said:

Sometimes I want the abrasive side and sometimes I want the other side, so you'll have to put the grips on both sides, and then the sponge wouldn't be big enough.

People have different size hands. I have very small hands and this is too big.

I have very big hands, would you make a small, medium, and large size?

Then they had another style where they lopped off all the corners. That was quickly dispatched. "How do I get into little spaces with this? I like to put my finger down in and smoosh it into corners when I'm cleaning. Don't take away my corners."

None of the shapes were any better, more practical, useful, sensible than what was already on the market. Essentially, what Chore Boy found out was that the selection the consumer has is just fine. There are more than enough shapes to make for happy housecleaning. Don't make it more complex, don't try to make it anything more than it is, don't give us unnecessary choices. A benefit has to have perceived meaning in the consumer's life, otherwise it's just another marketing ploy to be ignored. Let the consumer know what you're doing and how it will help him, and then see if he buys into the premise.

Another case in point: *Golf Digest*. The primary reason people buy any golf magazine is for the pros' tips, which golfers count on to miraculously transform their game. It's how they'll cut their handicap in half, put the power in their tee shot, the confidence in their putter. It's the stock in trade of all golf magazines. *Golf Digest* was looking for a way to stick out in the consumer's mind by offering a little something more. They would put small golfing icons in the corner of every tip to help readers identify what part of their game the tip was supposed to help. They designed an appropriate look for the icons and introduced the feature without fanfare into the magazine.

In the course of a readership study after the golf icons had been used for three years, none of the loyal readers I was speaking to ever mentioned those icons, even when I gave them the magazine to thumb through with the instructions to "tell me everything you're thinking as you typically read this magazine that you've been subscribing to for over 10 years." Nobody mentioned the icons unaided. I would point out the little symbol in the corner of the page that contained the tip. My respondent would start to chuckle.

Readers had pored over the magazine without the fleetest glance at—or consideration of—the graphics. They kept issues year after year to refer back to the tips, yet they had no idea what the symbols meant. By habit, golf fans knew how and where to find the magazine's tips and what part of their game they covered.

I recently picked up a copy of *Golf Digest*, and there on page 17, the same confusing symbols offered a "personalized guide to the tips," instructions to the instructions. Watch people at newsstands as they thumb through familiar magazines. They know how to instantly find their favorite features. Easier? How hard was it anyway?

LISTENING POINTS

- It's easier, cheaper, and less time-consuming to change a product than to change the consumer's mind.
- If you need detailed instructions about how to use a product, you probably need more work on your idea.
- Skilled eavesdropping provides more answers than direct questions.
- See your product through consumers' eyes. It has to make sense to them.
- The more you understand how the consumer lives, the more you will be able to deliver meaningful messages.
- Product benefits have to offer the consumer meaning and value.

7

CONSUMER LAMENTS

Learning from Consumer Disappointment

Winning customer loyalty is the brass ring; yet year in and year out, companies continue to do exactly the things that consumers complain about over and over again in focus groups. Everywhere along the business food chain, from manufacturing to marketing to merchandising, companies undermine their chances of gaining dedicated users by ignoring common consumer laments. They dilute the power of their own brand identity and then conduct more focus groups to find out where they went wrong. I've been doing this work for over 30 years and most of what's to follow has been irritating consumers for just as long.

Nuclear Proliferation

In the bad old days of the Soviet Union, we would see scenes of people lined up to enter stores with near barren shelves and product choices limited to one state-sponsored brand. How grateful, the subtext implied, we should be for our bounty of product possibilities. Remind yourself of that when you walk into the megadiscount store or supermarket to buy toothpaste or mustard and encounter football-field-length aisles, stacked six shelves high with toothpaste gels, pastes, brighteners, whiteners, sensitive, anticavity, antiplaque, antigingivitis, breath-freshening, striped, all-natural, mint-flavored options in travel, large, extralarge, and family sizes.

"*Stop!*" Consumers tell us repeatedly in focus groups. So many choices, so little difference, so much confusion. Instead of gaining loyalty, the exponential explosion within a brand encourages consumer fickleness. Proliferation for proliferation's sake is the kiss of death. Clients seeking shelf domination do it all the time. And they get the same negative message back from consumers. Instead of brands differentiating themselves from the competition, they're nuancing themselves out of customers' frame of consideration.

The cereal aisle today is a shopper's Tower of Babel. The shopper combs the aisles armed with a fistful of supermarket coupons simply looking for packages with colors and graphics that match the pictures on the coupons in her hand. The cereal companies are easily seduced by the licensing trap. If Pokémon is hot, they come out with a Pokémon cereal. But when Pokémon dies, nobody wants it anymore. The kids' cereals that endure have characters tied to the brand instead of to whatever is trendy: Captain Crunch, the Fruit Loops parrot, the Trix rabbit.

Whenever there are so many choices out there, the consumer either doesn't care anymore or just gets mad. To further aggravate parents, sugar-saturated cereals (pushed in Saturday morning kid-TV fare) have a place of honor on bottom shelves, eye level for children. Mothers resent the brands and often claim that they only buy them under duress, with a screaming child in tow. Now, if a cereal can get one iota of market share the manufacturer is ecstatic but the buyer isn't likely to be all that brand loyal.

Above all, customers want simplicity and convenience. Marketers just continue to pile stuff on the shelf because rumor has it that the consumer is making more and more decisions there. Everybody competes to get as much real estate on the shelf as possible without considering the consequences of brand diffusion.

Maybe you've had an experience like this one: I just left the supermarket in confusion, and this is my business. I was looking for chocolate Ensure for my mother. First I saw a brown box saying chocolate Ensure. Okay, but wait, there was another brown box, chocolate Ensure with calcium. Well what was the first Ensure? Vitamin D. Did that mean it has no calcium? Then I saw one with protein. But did that mean it doesn't have calcium either? Another box said "enriched, fortified." I wondered, what is it fortified with? Is it the one with both calcium and protein? In the end, I left with a bottle of Centrum Silver multivitamins and some store brand calcium supplements, and decided my mother would be better off with water. None of the Ensure formulas fit the bill. Marketers have really got to learn this. They have to make it simple, simple, simple. Time Warner didn't come out with a magazine called *Real Simple* for no reason. Someone's getting the message.

What manufacturers sometimes misunderstand from research is that when the consumer says, "I'm looking for something simple," it may mean "I have it already. You don't need to give it to me." What's simple is buying an apple and having it in the morning. That doesn't mean I want you to take fruit, put it in a bag, charge me 10 times as much as for an apple, and not have it taste as good as an apple. But if you give me an apple-flavored snack that I can keep in my car for three weeks without having it spoil, then you've also given me the added value of convenience and just maybe I'll consider it.

We're all time pressured and stressed out. We do want things to be easy, but we want things to work well and be of reasonable quality. Sometimes manufacturers have thought that if a product is convenient, the consumer will forgo other things. For example, frozen chicken cacciatore doesn't have to taste as good as mama's homemade chicken cacciatore because it's merely a convenience product. Well, these days consumers don't compromise as much, and they won't compromise strictly for convenience. Convenience is just a tiebreaker. Convenience works when the consumer doesn't have the time or the inclination or the necessary utensils. But the consumer still wants something that has quality, and brands like Stouffer's, Lean Cuisine, and Marie Callender have recognized this. They have offered added value along the way so the consumer isn't left with a confusing array of selections. Stouffer's has big portions, side dishes, family size. Lean Cuisine offers up great gourmet—like variety in an ever-changing menu of choice as long as their kitchens can successfully put it in a box without sacrificing the taste and texture of the final product. Marie Callender has packaged the aura of homemade comfort foods and traditional blue-plate specials. Marie Callender might not be gourmet, but she's got the market nailed on a turkey dinner with all the fixings in a way that a Swanson's TV dinner hasn't been able to approach.

Some products are simple and convenient already. Others cry out for simplification, particularly in product selection—which doesn't always mean take all your products off the shelf and just have one. Robitussin packaged its various cough syrup formulations in different colors to make it easier for consumers to find the right carton. It's nice if the consumer knows your brand; it's still okay if he can identify you with a particular color. But when generic brands come along and copy the packaging, you're back with the same problem, or worse.

Hair coloring screams for simplification. Clairol had come up with so many different brands that the only people who could tell the difference were the people who worked for Clairol. Brand advertisement was inconsistent. In the days of TV's *Dynasty*, you'd see commercials for Ultress with Linda Evans, and the consumer knew that this was probably expensive, fancier somehow. Then she wouldn't see any advertising for Ultress for a while, and it would come back with commercials that talked about how the coloring was a gel and therefore less drippy.

Clairol wanted to do some research that would help them get out of this mess. I talked to women who regularly used coloring throughout the country and asked how they perceived hair color. If they were going to categorize it, how would they sort them? Consumers looked at me dumbfounded. These were experienced users who had worked through the complexities, and they did know the difference. And they kept saying, "It's sort of like A-B-C, or 1-2-3. Doesn't last very long, lasts a little longer, lasts a long time." And after 10 minutes with each focus group, the answer was the same.

As a result, Clairol took all their brands and labeled them, drum roll . . . "1, 2, or 3," depending on how long the color lasted. Any brand marked 1 would be the most temporary, like Loving Care—wash in, wash out. And within each of these categories, the consumer could pick the brand that she wanted. Simple to use, not intimidating, not threatening.

Clairol did more than simplify the process. By talking and then listening to the hair color veterans, they learned how to talk to those women who are on the bubble about coloring their hair. Clairol had assumed that everybody knew you get a bottle, you may need to add another bottle to it, then you take that, you put it on your head for a certain period of time, you rinse it off, you use a little conditioner so your hair won't be damaged, you let it dry, and you're home free. Your hair looks great.

But people who have never colored their hair don't know that. Maybe they saw their mother trapped in a bathroom swathed in towels, dripping black gook down her face, looking at her watch, waiting for the minute she would be able to get the stuff off. People need information to make decisions. Tell them what's going on and maybe you can reach someone at that crucial moment of decision. For Clairol, that woman is at the shelf thinking "should I?" The way to tip the balance is to reassure her that this is no big deal, and if she doesn't like it, the color's out in a couple of washings. The implication to begin with gentler number 1 may cut through all this indecision.

Tinkering with a Brand

We all know the classic example—the Classic Coke example, that is. Coca-Cola asked America to replace their Classic Coke with New Coke and America en masse just said no. New and improved wouldn't fly when the old and reliable was just fine. To its drinkers, original Coke lived on sacred ground, a territory shared by few products. Why mess with a winning brand and put a relationship at risk? Soft drink fans weren't clamoring for the next new thing, but a lag in sales convinced Coke executives that the problem might call for a change in formula. Hearing the rising panic, Coke quenched the thirst of cola junkies by resurrecting the original and marketing the imposter overseas, where presumably they weren't as dedicated to one formulation of the American icon.

We're creatures of habit, reluctant to disrupt our familiar patterns, so there needs to be a good reason for tinkering. Often the real reason a brand tries something new isn't consumer demand but a boss's demand for increased sales or a new manager's desperate effort to make an impression. Innovation and forward thinking are fine but not at the expense of alienating core customers.

For years, Jell-O has had a box with a bag of the powder mix inside it. One day, Jell-O realized they could probably save money on each box if they took that useless bag out and just put the Jell-O in the box. Their thinking was, what's the big deal anyhow? The bag isn't really necessary. Boxing has improved so much over the years that you don't need that double packaging. If they just put the stuff in the box, it would be fine.

The plan was hatched and we made up a batch of boxes without the bag inside and gave it to people to try. We told them it was a new product, use it the way you normally would. (When doing packaging studies, you don't want to say this is a new package. You want to get as close to real use as possible.) The test consumers came back furious. They were used to tearing open the box, then opening up the bag and pouring out the powder. But, because there was no bag, when they opened up the box with their usual fervor, the Jell-O powder flew all over the kitchen. Needless to say, the company bagged the concept.

Frequent, unnecessary model revisions get consumers steamed. Sure Americans love new things, but we understand the difference between new and better and change designed to jack up the price.

I used to do research for Playtex. What a lot of griping I used to hear in lingerie groups as women grumbled that just as they located the perfect-fit bra, they couldn't find it anymore. Women tend to stockpile their favorite model bra in defense against its inevitable disappearance. Playtex's 800-number probably attests to this ongoing consumer anger. If I were Playtex, I'd keep models in stock for a certain span of years, like car manufacturers do, and invite my loyalists to get in touch with me via e-mail when they're ready to reorder.

Consumers often scratch their heads at features companies deem important. Delivering on fundamental consumer needs and understanding the relative importance of those needs should be uppermost in marketing minds. Too many brands focus on coming up with frivolous extras instead of improving the basic product or service in meaningful ways.

I conducted groups with owners of small businesses for MCI (before it was MCI WorldCom, and before wireless communication was on the horizon). Customers then were moaning about the labyrinth of calling plans. They despised the incessant solicitation to switch long-distance companies. They wanted simplicity, but this item wasn't on MCI's agenda. Instead, the company had designed an exciting new technology that they felt would offer their small business customers added value.

One thing the technology could do was rearrange charges to cluster certain items. In the same way that American Express offered significant added value to its members some years ago when they made quarterly reports available with breakdowns for lodging, air travel, car rental, retail purchases, and so forth, the MCI thinking was to allow consumers to code in numbers according to who in the company was placing the call or according to the function of the call.

Interesting, but complicated was the judgment from small business owners. The response: "In the scheme of running a small business, this type of minutiae really isn't going to save me time or money. Can't you think of something that will simplify my life?" Small businesses tend to treat their phone bills the way we deal with them at home. They scan the bill to see if there are any outrageous amounts, look at the details of those calls, remember the circumstances, and go on. The bill might be a point of difference between MCI and its competitors, but it was a fairly irrelevant one.

In the same arena, when I did work for Bell South about cellular phone plans and rates, customers were yearning for a single source phone company. What had been busted up into hundreds of Baby Bells in the 1970s, was now a royal pain in the neck in the 1990s, and consumers were eager to get a single bill for local service, long distance, cellular, and even equipment and service fees. Where once we worried about the monopoly of utilities, it now seemed like a pretty good alternative for a simpler life.

Manufacturers play with package sizes and come up with new shapes and containers that consumers take home and then can't fit it on their standard size shelves. It took refrigerators a while to catch up with the two-liter plastic bottle for soft drinks. At first it had to be laid on its side next to the leftover potato salad; now it fits in your refrigerator door.

Post cereals knew that rival Quaker was starting to market some of its cereals in bags without boxes, and wondered what it would gain them if they went this same route. The bag in the box of cereal does have a function: It keeps the cereal fresher. When you use cereal, you fold down the bag and close it up. But that bag is glued to the sides in such a way that when you fold it down it usually lifts off from the sides and cereal tends to fall between the bag and the box. It's a nuisance, so consumers have a love/hate relationship with the interior bag in a box of cereal.

Post had listened to this over and over in focus groups and said: "Let's eliminate the box and just give them a bag. We'll make it out of a stronger material. Consumers are down on excess packaging anyhow." Ergo, they designed packaging that would really help keep the cereal fresh. One had a zip lock closure after you opened it, and the other was a turn-down, with a piece of metal that wrapped around the bag.

As it turned out, one of the most important things for the consumer was storage consideration. Rectangular boxes fit nicely in cabinets and consumers know how to handle them, whereas bags collapse. The cereal would have to be put in a different place if Post changed the packaging shape.

Ultimately, Post was asking consumers to make a lot of changes in what right now is a mindless act and consider an aspect of a product that they never really thought about before. Nor were they passing on huge savings, as were other manufacturers who had put their cereal in bags. The bag cereals that had been successful were more likely to be generic brands purchased primarily for price consideration. Post wasn't ready to back down on price. To consumers, there seemed to be a lot of compromises and no added value. It was pretty much of a bust.

Uncle Ben's introduced convenience meals in bowls, which are wonderful to eat out of but a storage nightmare. When I heard consumers talking about it in groups, they thought it was a bit of a rip-off in terms of price, because the bowl was really pretty small. Still someone in that company knew how to listen because Uncle Ben's put the small round bowl in a large square, easy-to-store-in-the-freezer package.

In terms of packaging, deciphering labels shouldn't require a course in semiotics or an updated prescription for your reading glasses. Seniors, for example, are terribly frustrated—and may even be endangered—by tiny print on over-the-counter medicines. It's also exasperating for them when they can't read a model or size number because it's worn off in the wash.

The label is valuable territory, but it won't sell the product for you unless the information is well mapped out and the words have real meaning for the busy shopper. Pepperidge Farm finally realized that they had to differentiate their various chocolate chip goodies by explanations and banners of color as well as by names of small American towns like Sausalito and Montauk.

The shopping aisle provides another roadblock. Watch customers try to navigate narrow supermarket aisles congested with shopping carts. I did a job for Sears when they were rethinking their maternity department and talked to expectant mothers, whose distaste for small, crammed departments ran in inverse proportion to the size of their bellies. They want space, big dressing rooms, wide aisles, room to move around. Don't make it too hot and be sure there's a bathroom close by. Pregnant women were rallying for functional considerations rather than cuddly fleece toys and montages of cute babies.

As mentioned, parents seethe at the lineup of sugar-laced cereal placed precisely at kids' grabbing level, while seniors complain at having to bend down too low to reach their preferences. Shoppers don't want to peruse every can of soup before spotting mushroom because the cans aren't in alphabetical order. Consumers are hip to what's going on down the aisle, and they know when it's not organized for their convenience.

Advertising Truths

Advertising is the public personality of a brand. It supplies helpful, if at times limited, information; and the American public readily accepts advertising as part of the tariff. We applaud the effort when it's good. Don't Super Bowl ads entertain far more than the halftime show and often more than the game itself? We've passed from asking "where's the beef?" to "whasssup?" Ads featuring the Zelig-like Absolut vodka bottle frequently seem to be the most ingenious pages in a magazine. Although the campaign has been going on forever—there's even a coffee-table book of Absolut ads—each incarnation feels fresh and new. Still the perception lingers that we hate advertising. What we really dislike are the condescension, deceptiveness, stereotyping, puffery, rival bashing, arrogance, obtuseness of many ads. And what annoys us the most is the notion that someone is trying to put one over on us.

Since I often test concepts before they're foisted on the general public, I repeatedly find advertisers lack a real understanding of their intended customer. Consumers pick up on it instantly.

Some of the most blatant examples arise when one gender is involved in intimate products meant for the other. Women probably won't ever understand what it's really like for a man to shave his face every morning; men who haven't worn pantyhose can't understand the importance of the right crotch fit.

Playtex was trying to develop relevant advertising for its new baby feeding system. I showed a commercial, which had a baby crying in the background, to new mothers. All the women were nursing, and as I looked around the room, I saw faces in stunned disbelief. The problem: Never show a wailing infant to nursing mothers because they'll begin to secrete milk. The sound of a crying baby stimulates the mammary glands. I don't know who created the ad, but I'm reasonably certain it wasn't a young mom. Playtex had a great product that's now beloved by new mothers, but they would have had an irate group at their doorstep had they released the original ad.

How many times have you looked at an ad, couldn't figure out what it was trying to sell you, and turned the page in protest? A brand of premium supermarket coffee was trying to avoid further sales shrinkage by using a more modern billboard campaign, à la Altoids, and decided to push the image of the essence of coffee. One proposed billboard had two pairs of feet sticking out of a bed and a tiny can of the coffee brand. No coffee cup, no spoon, no tray with flowers, no nothing.

"Is it sexual?" someone asked (as with most advertising, sort of). "What are they trying to communicate? What does coffee have to do with sex? I don't get it."

"I would never drink coffee in bed," someone else chimed in. "It would spill."

They could have at least had a breakfast tray with a half-filled cup. Consumers pick up on so many visual signals and clues these days. A half-full cup of coffee indicates somebody had some, so it must be good. And a couple of crumbs on a breakfast tray shows human involvement. This had none of it and neither would coffee drinkers.

The slew of puzzling commercials during dot.com mania had more than a few people puzzling over what in the world these companies were even advertising.

An upshot of the Internet revolution was that every company decided it had to position itself on the cutting edge of dot.com contemporary global thinking. In that pursuit, a major Fortune 100 player had their agency develop a corporate print campaign that would be aimed at CFOs, CEOs, and executive VP types, a relatively conservative middle-aged demographic. The campaign print ads featured trendy typefaces; every other word was a different style and font so it looked like a chic graphics magazine.

We talked to the kind of men who were going to be reading this. These poor guys had no idea of what was going on. They couldn't even read it. Once we realized this campaign wasn't going to work, the agency didn't get all bent out of shape. They had heard the problem, and went back to work to develop one that didn't require a graffiti artist to decipher. As a bonus, we learned a lot more about this audience and how to reach them, which is what qualitative research is all about.

LISTENING POINTS

◉ Proliferation creates confusion.

◉ A disappointed consumer is hard to reclaim.

◉ Convenience by itself isn't a sufficient selling point.

◉ Consumers don't like to break their habits so don't tinker with your brand unless you have to.

◉ Make your point quickly. Consumer attention span is very short.

◉ Inference sells, abstraction obfuscates.

◉ You're in trouble if the consumer has to work at the aisle to make a decision.

8

BRAND STANDING

Uncovering the True Identity of a Brand

Part of my job is to get clients out of their day-to-day consumption of sales data and into the less tangible, more abstract world of branding and brand essence or brand footprint. Once you assess and understand your brand, and recognize what being a brand means, you're better able to gauge where you can go and what you can do. You can make informed decisions about how to maintain a loyal customer base, attract new consumers, move into new product areas, or respond to the competition.

In the early days of marketing, brands were primarily a simple means of identification. Let's use soap pads as an example: There were pink ones and blue ones. So, when consumers heard Brillo, they were supposed to think "pink pad." The main characteristic or attribute of Brillo was its pinkness. These traits were how brands differentiated one from the other. Move ahead and what was once only a shorthand for characteristics (pink vs. blue) evolved into marketers' realization that they could gain more ground if they massaged the characteristic to represent a benefit.

What does pink stand for? Enhanced grease-cutting power was pretty viable, and so that became the new value of buying Brillo, the pink pad.

A brand identity differentiates your corner green market from A&P, your neighborhood copy shop from Kinko's, and even your local junior college from New York University. Other companies sell cards, but how likely are you to name one besides Hallmark? What do cows and computers have in common? Nothing really, but Gateway computers' cow-splotched boxes helped it stand out from the rest of the PC herd. The whimsical packaging created a folksy, down-home image, particularly appealing to the techno-shy. The product inside the box worked well, too, and if it didn't, Gateway promised to provide reliable service and tech support. As a consequence of this Silicon Prairie approach, Gateway forged a unique identity in a category dominated at the time by the notion that computers were pretty much the same.

Brands have the same flat personae as celebrities—we don't actually know Madonna but we can ascribe a group of traits to her. Madonna is also a very different brand from Julie Andrews, but they are both viable, easy-to-remember brands. The care and feeding of a brand identity takes time and vision, but if you're not working toward defining your attributes and making sure that customers understand what makes you unique, you may be building generic awareness of the category for someone else. Checking in with the consumer allows you to identify areas of strength to exploit and weaknesses that require adjustment.

Brand Matters

Despite its name, French's mustard is perceived as an all-American fun, family brand. Any consideration of breaking into the gourmet mustard world works against that image. The brand's core customers made it clear to us that they weren't going to make the leap up with French's. They saw French's as a yellow, squeeze-bottle mustard. French's answer to Grey Poupon and Maille and other fancier sounding, sharper tasting flavors had to be in keeping with that image. French's realized that as long as a big part of its brand footprint was family and kids, they could come out with a host of exotic flavors but in milder versions, never stronger than the product it's eaten with.

After *TV Guide* was purchased by Gemstar, I was asked to do creativity sessions in Los Angeles among a core group of brand user loyalists to find out, Could the brand, that big brand, stand for all the different businesses *TV Guide* was entering? Would a brand that was so identified as that little book sitting next to the remote be able to support interactive selection of programs, the Web page, TiVo, the convergence of different media, all the electronic developments and anything else coming down the line? How can *TV Guide* continue to be a meaningful brand? Would consumers in the next 10 years feel that a television set is only a monitor or that television programming itself is only a part of some larger and more complex entertainment-information category? Big questions for an established brand like *TV Guide* to be pondering.

Rightly so, they decided to involve the consumer in the process about how *TV Guide* could evolve and continue to be relevant. The consumer perspective yielded wonderful insights into the brand. I asked if *TV Guide* were a celebrity, a country, a Los Angeles neighborhood, a TV show, who or what would it be? The comments revealed the power of this brand:

> It's like Jerusalem because it's been there since the beginning of time.
>
> It's your grandmother's plant; what you remember on top of the television set when you were five years old.
>
> It's like the frozen foods aisle: everything is just waiting there at your finger tips, you just have to reach out and get it.

> It's the United Nations, takes all separate elements and puts them together and allows them to exist as one entity.
>
> It's Princess Di, she helped to guide a lot of people.

The projective exercises painted the *TV Guide* brand as familiar as an old slipper, yet with an endearing quirkiness and authoritativeness. It provided fantastic guidance that could help viewers make choices in a tangible way.

The prevailing image that everybody loved was that of the Sherpa. The Sherpa is more than a safari guide; the Sherpa is the guy who has some inside knowledge that you need. This person is going to get you there. You just trust him and you rely on him. In this same way, users trust and rely on *TV Guide*. The viewer doesn't have to know anything else except that it's in *TV Guide*. You always know if it says it's going to be on at 8:00 P.M., it's going to be on at 8:00 P.M. If it says it's going to be the episode where grandpa loses his teeth, you know it's not going to be the one where grandma learns to drive. If it's out of its realm, it doesn't venture a guess. There's an inherent honesty to *TV Guide*.

Still relevant, still accessible, still helpful. When you hear words like trust, authentic, honest as part of your brand's footprint, fireworks should go off because you've hit the marketing jackpot. For *TV Guide*, that means it should continue to build on this brand awareness with image advertising that reinforces its relevance in people's lives and emphasizes its ability to help make choices regardless of the medium. As the entertainment world turns, *TV Guide* is going to be there to help you sort through this confusing array of possibilities. Like the Sherpa.

This direction was a huge departure from what some of the *TV Guide* honchos had in mind for it. They wanted to take *TV Guide* "Hollywood," make it glitzier. After all this valuable information emerged, I sat around with the *TV Guide* executives. At first, everybody was all excited. They decided they should develop a brand trust office. They acknowledged that they were busy and involved in typical day-to-day, tactical areas, but ultimately the most important thing for them to pursue and stay on top of was the brand. It had to be nurtured, it had to be cherished, it had to be portrayed in the right way.

Then, as so often happens, they got involved in short-term decisions such as trying to figure out if the red *TV Guide* logo could be used as ornaments on a Christmas tree for the year's holiday card. (The design team was holding the presses until my clients in Los Angeles made a decision.) As time passed, they lost sight of brand as they began to worry about the content portion of their interactive business. How big should the top part of the screen be? How much editorializing should they incorporate? These are important and necessary decisions, but all too often, they overshadow due brand diligence, and the beauty of that Sherpa imagery fades. I don't get the feeling a few years later that they're pursuing this valuable brand equity. And my fear about the brand is that it's going to lapse out. When all of this media convergence happens, this brand may not be prepared, which would be a shame because they have so much going for it as the authentic voice for home viewers of the world of entertainment.

At some point, another brand may come along and take advantage of the lull to woo consumers. Just recently on a business trip to Los Angeles I caught a glimpse of a commercial with Jason Alexander, full face to the camera, extolling the virtues of *DirecTV* magazine, with a Sherpa-like tag line that conveyed a sense of this brand's ability to help you make the right choices. Wake up, *TV Guide*. There's another Sherpa company on the mountain. (The latest rumor has it that *TV Guide* will simply gobble up the competition, a viable strategy they've followed in the past.)

And yet, the day-to-day stewards of the *TV Guide* brand can't really be faulted. Gemstar wants a healthy bottom line and short-term tactics with offers of extended subscriptions for 50 percent off newsstand price sell the product. Brand nurturing is a long-term project. The tangible evidence of success is slow to build. But the ultimate rewards are solid and meaningful. The bottom line is ultimately bigger, better, and stronger. It just takes patience, commitment, and focus.

A few years ago, New York University officials began to consider what attributes caused current students to choose the school. As the Department of Advertising and Publications was preparing to issue a new "beauty book"—the brochure sent to prospective applicants—for the School of Social Work, it dawned on them that some focus groups could be designed to find out from students what about NYU had attracted them to the school rather than to any other college. My NYU clients rightfully assumed that an ad in *The New York Times* on Sunday wasn't enough to lure potential enrollees; they had to find a unique position in the college marketplace. What did the NYU School of Social Work brand stand for? What set it apart from its competition—the Ivy League Columbia or Fordham with its Catholic identity.

NYU began the study believing that the main points of differentiation were that it offered more hands-on clinical work, a really good balance of academic and clinical fieldwork. We interviewed people who had gone to NYU, and they all said sure, that's why they had chosen the university. But the more we asked about their experiences and listened, the more we heard that the underlying reason was the specific cachet of NYU, the feel of the school. It had a homeyness despite being in New York City, the sensibility of a smaller, special place. A good education was expected. The key for NYU was to emphasize the appeal of its villagelike character that makes the university stand out, in other words, its brand.

The conventional wisdom used to say people chose the supermarket they shopped in because it was close. It was location, location, location. Then in areas like southern Florida when large national chains like Albertson's and King Kullen started setting up shop in the same location, Publix Supermarkets thought there might be more to attracting customers than placement along a well-traveled artery. Likewise, if they were going to spend money to advertise, there might be better tactics than specials of the week—lettuce 99 cents and buy one Minute Maid get the second one free.

They were right. As we listened to people who shopped at Publix describe how they felt about it, what they liked about Publix and what that store represented to them versus others, we realized how much went into that experience. It was a real eye-opener.

This particular study was conducted 20 years ago, and the value of brand cachet for supermarket chains is common knowledge now. Publix, however, was the first to understand that shoppers form conclusions about a store by observing how clean the floors are, by noticing the attitude of the employees, by seeing how easy it is to navigate the aisles with a shopping cart, by being able to locate products in the same aisle every time, and by finding the shelves being fully stocked out to the front. These distinctions were pluses for Publix and bad news for other stores.

Until then, supermarkets hadn't really been thinking of themselves as a true brand, but the more we talked about supermarkets and the more we asked people in focus groups to imagine themselves in different stores, and tell us how they were feeling—the emotional component of pushing a cart through aisles filled with products and other shoppers—the more we learned how important the supermarket brand identity was. It wasn't just price, service, wide aisles, and piped-in music. It was how customers felt when they walked into that store. The combination of tangible and intangible elements contributed to a more pleasurable shopping experience and raised the standing of the Publix brand to the extent that shoppers told us that they got more dressed up to go out for their groceries at that store.

Pockets of resistance remain in the brand onslaught. Name a brand of peat moss or pool chemical, for instance. Brand may be less relevant in certain commodity categories like milk and eggs, and generally people have less to say about them. On the other hand, this is changing and any and all products should be trying to understand the inherent value of their brand. When there is hardly any differentiation in a category, this may very well represent an opportunity for one brand to establish a beachhead and profit from taking the high ground by creating an identity that consumers can relate to. I could be persuaded to always seek out a particular brand of peat moss, if there were a brand that stood for planting success, or a swimming pool chemical that I believed was an authority on clarity and safety.

Most fruits and vegetables used to fit the commodity mold. Generally, only produce like pineapples (Dole) and bananas (Chiquita), grown in and imported from limited geographic locales, had recognizable brands. Today, the produce aisle looks a lot different. Lettuce is bagged and branded. Oranges are stamped and apples are tagged. As this trend was just dawning, one citrus brand, figuring it could take advantage of its domination in produce, looked into establishing a brand presence for pistachio nuts. They could do oranges; why not go nuts?

They asked me to check out the potential of branded pistachios, but first, they had to understand "the pistachio gestalt." The client wanted its brand to stand for quality and nut superiority. What does that mean with reference to a pistachio nut? Would people care more about a brand name or where pistachio nuts come from? What do consumers know about them now? So we talked to a lot of people in Los Angeles, Chicago, Boston, and the New York suburbs, all of who had personally purchased and consumed pistachio nuts within the past year. We talked to them about the perfect nut, about pistachio nuts in the big realm of snacks, about red versus natural. They defined the personality of a pistachio: healthy, into exercise, unpretentious, analytical, individualistic, easygoing, well educated, intelligent, creative, patient, relaxed, male rather than female. All very interesting stuff.

Then we talked to them about using the client's logo on each nut. That's when we lost them. Most panelists agreed that it would be silly to have people or machines stamping little marks or putting tiny stickers on each nut. Instead of engendering warm, fuzzy feelings about the product, consumers viewed the idea as a supreme waste of time and energy. This go-round, the client was unable to translate its brand into anything meaningful for consumers when it came to bulk pistachios, but Nabisco's Mr. Peanut had to start somewhere too.

It takes time and patience to penetrate the consumer's heart and mind. As the competition for customers' attention intensifies, fewer and fewer areas can remain brand blank slates. Like Publix, smart companies seize the opportunity to create a powerful brand from a strong product or service. Establishing brand awareness in areas not traditionally brand oriented can prove a significant competitive stroke.

Tyvek™, a building wrap trademarked by Du Pont, was able to do that by leapfrogging over its immediate customers in the construction trade to create awareness among home buyers.

Du Pont plastered the Tyvek name all over the sheets of wrap, turning them into an instant if inadvertent billboard.

Du Pont hired me to see if and how Tyvek registered among consumers. In groups, I'd ask how many had heard of Tyvek. "Tyvek, oh yeah, that's out on that home going up down on Route 413. I don't know what it is, but you see it up there on that big old house." Du Pont had created awareness for its product in a category where there had been none, getting a huge competitive leg up on its rivals. Moreover, home buyers linked Tyvek with sound construction. People would pass by houses under construction sheathed in this stuff that said Tyvek, Tyvek, Tyvek and often weren't even sure what its purpose was, they just associated it with better homes and they wanted it.

When we spoke to builders, they said that they take their cues from home owners. Builders confirmed that they too benefited from Du Pont's marketing effort to the extent that they tried to make sure that the Tyvek trademark was right side up as they stapled it. When manufacturers advertise a brand, builders can turn around and boast to the home buyers about using the product. Anderson did the same thing with windows. Anderson is not necessarily the best window—it's a well-manufactured window at a mid-range price—but it's done so much promotion aimed at home owners that builders now say, "I only use Anderson windows" as their own selling point. "Come home to Anderson." Can you hum the jingle?

Brand Stature

As with celebrities, brands are not of equal stature and they drift in and out of favor. Taking occasional stock of a brand's status alerts you to signs that its star is fading as the competitive environment shifts or consumer priorities change. Or it tells you that like a Grade B actor, the brand is not capable of supporting anything bigger.

In 1993, the warning signs were 20-foot high neon when I was asked to be part of a team hired to help the Hard Rock Cafe understand its brand identity. Once upon a time, the Hard Rock was an exciting, underground, word-of-mouth place in an out-of-the-way location. The original had opened in 1971, in a swinging London. By the late 1980s, Hard Rock Cafes had multiplied throughout the world and become about as hip as JCPenney.

When we interviewed consumers, again and again they told us that the food sucked and once you got that ubiquitous T-shirt, why go back? We talked to young people who had been to the Hard Rock in their hometown (e.g., the Dallas Hard Rock), and then we branched out and spoke to tourists who had recently visited one not in their hometown. This was a recruiting challenge. We managed to get a handful of tourists in New York City around Columbus Day because the Hard Rock Cafe cooperated and let us through to ask our screening questions.

If you walked across Fifty-seventh Street, you'd see that the velvet ropes of Planet Hollywood were being stampeded by the young and the hip. Considerably less busy, the doorman at Hard Rock Cafe had time to stop by Planet Hollywood to get one of the free cups of coffee they were offering the hoards of line standers on that cold day.

Then we went to London where our recruiters almost got arrested for asking questions, clipboard in hand, of tourists queued up to see the Royal Jewels. And we went to Berlin right after the fall of the Wall where the fading image of the Hard Rock Cafe really hit home. My friend and colleague Karen Weilhusen, of Kompass Research, did the groups in German, and I was on hand if respondents seemed more conversant in English. The only tourists we could get in Berlin who had recently been to the Hard Rock there were Turkish teenagers who were equally enchanted and delighted with the likes of MTV (the Internet was only a glimpse in the eyes of the most computer savvy at this time).

No matter who the panelists, the brand continued to stand for fading rockers, crummy food, and the place you got the T-shirt. And, that's exactly what we told the Hard Rock management. "If you continue to think that you're drawing in crowds based on their eagerness to see some old rock star's guitar, you're in trouble. If you remain static, you're heading toward irrelevance." We advised them to think about moving the Hard Rock Cafe brand in other directions and at the very least to do something about that godawful food.

My colleague M. L. Sirianni had collage boards developed to capture all the different directions that the Hard Rock brand could take. We showed these boards around the United States and in London and Berlin. The brand could stand for really great comfort food, late night, musician food. The brand could stand for global communication; youth around the world could be persuaded to flock to the Hard Rock as a means of cyberspace communication. M. L. was really ahead of her time on this one. I remember how turned on the young panelists in all cities were to think that with a click of some button they'd be able to tune into the crowd at a Hard Rock in Milan or San Antonio.

In addition to comfort food and hip cyber communication, there were at least four or five other positionings for the brand to think about. We reported the results to the then management in Orlando, who could only hear the cell phones in the conference room alerting them to brushfires that really needed tending to. So they thought.

The Hard Rock Cafe management at the time didn't want to hear anything about being a brand. They were convinced that brands only related to packaged goods and other tangible products that were sold on supermarket shelves and consumed. The Hard Rock Cafe was not a brand, we were advised.

Frequently, when the news is painful, the armor against the truth grows stronger. Management refused to accept our recommendations because they thought they could continue to feed on the past glory of the original. Not long after, when the signs of impending disaster were absolutely overwhelming, new management finally began to broaden the Hard Rock franchise. They ignored the brushfires and started tending to the major brand conflagration.

Today, most remaining theme restaurants are limping along on life support, but Hard Rock has moved into hotel, television, recording, and concert businesses as a natural extension of its music-themed restaurants. The Hard Rock Cafe brand does, indeed, stand for more than buildings where people go to buy T-shirts.

Transforming a Brand

Just changing your product doesn't mean the consumer will feel differently about the brand. As Snapple was overhauling the cold beverage category, resuscitating iced tea by making it available in a convenient, glass, single-serve, portable bottle, Nestea, popular only as a dry mix in canisters, was developing its own new way to package and deliver a fresh brewed iced tea taste. Nestea's approach was to sell the tea in the refrigerated section, next to orange juice and milk, in what marketers call a gable-top wax cardboard container (what we know as a milk container).

All of their quantitative testing had confirmed that it was a delicious tasting tea. It scored higher than any of its competition, including Snapple. When consumers blind-tested it by the glassful, they gave the brew lip-smacking endorsements, indicating they would be favorably inclined to buy the new product. It would cost considerably more than the powder, but roughly the same as Snapple. The manufacturer thought that all they needed was a clever way of talking about the new product, a positioning that would provide a meaningful reason why the Nestea refrigerated tea should be purchased and had greater value.

In our sessions, panelists dismissed the entire premise. The key reason was the Nestea brand itself. Snapple was the new kid on the block. At the time, the brand was hip, just arrogant enough. No matter how hard we tried to talk about Nestea as a great-tasting iced tea now available in the refrigerated section, the consumer had removed the Nestea brand so far from tea that it had its own little place . . . bellywash, cheap, convenient, and something you make by the Hummer-load. Nestea would have a hard time rising above its unsophisticated, low-end, image. Anything the brand wanted to say about fresh brewed taste landed on deaf ears. Nestea would have a lot of trouble becoming the premium-priced, great-tasting, ready-to-drink fresh-brewed adult iced tea in the refrigerated section.

Transforming a brand is tough going once it's etched into consumer consciousness. It's hard to wipe out a strong image. But if you have no brand image, the world is your oyster. You can make yourself be whatever you want.

About a decade ago, when Amazon.com was not on the lips of every reader, the book world consisted of a couple of mall-based stores (primarily Waldenbooks and B. Dalton), wonderful independent stores still managing to hang on in major cities, and the emerging Borders and Barnes & Noble superstores, which had copied the groundbreaking *sofa-and-easy chair, drink-coffee-and-read-the-books-and-magazines-if-you-want-to concepts* of stores like The Tattered Cover in Denver.

Having marketed the Borders stores, which were big and comfortable and hugely successful, Waldenbooks didn't know what to do with its core brand. In 1995, they hired a bright marketing executive to decide what it should stand for, to find a positioning for the store. As opposed to Hard Rock Cafe, at least Waldenbooks recognized that the name was more than a glass-doored presence in malls. They suspected that the Waldenbooks brand had no image, and while top management saw this as a major problem, in my mind, that represented a tremendous opportunity.

The situation with Waldenbooks was that when they started in malls everybody was hot into the malls. As an afterthought, while people shopped and hung out at malls they went to Waldenbooks. At the time, their archrival was B. Dalton. I don't know who came first, B. Dalton or Waldenbooks, but neither was faring well. In the consumer's mind, they were interchangeable, which tends to happen with mall stores. Adding to their woes, malls themselves had lost their mystique and entertainment value, at least for adults. To get a read on what Waldenbooks was and could be, we went to Philadephia, Denver, and Seattle.

What I discovered was that the store's image, indeed, was nonexistent. People weren't seeing Waldenbooks and saying, "Phooey, horrible, I want nothing to do with that store." But neither was it a destination that people specifically went to. They were saying, "Oh, it's called B. Walton's, right, it's in the mall. I remembered I had to pick up a gift for my son's teacher so I went in there when I was in the mall."

Waldenbooks needed a clear motivating positioning. With books in its name, it had a perfect base. The message could be Waldenbooks is books and only books. They could have said we're not about atmosphere, we're not about ambience, we're not about easy chairs, if you like books come to us, we've got books. If this was to be the positioning, then it would have to be very focused. They would truly have to communicate that Waldenbooks will do anything you want for books. We'll find them, order them, and ship them. They could have been the book kings, the premise that Amazon, then in its neonatal stage, used as its jumping-off point.

Catering to the special needs of parents was another area they could explore. Parents with their children populate malls, and mothers are always looking for places to park the kids. Mothers have specific considerations. The kids' section has to be near a bathroom. There should be only one way in and one way out of the children's part of the store. They want an area where they could be browsing at Mary Higgins Clark and glance over and know that their child isn't running free and about to go out into the mall. If you're really good at this, the kids are going to say, I want to go to Waldenbooks, mothers are going to be happy to oblige, and you're continuing to pound home your brand.

They could have specialized in children under the age of five. If Waldenbooks had said come to WaldenKids for the best selection of children's books, they would have won parents over. Or they could have enhanced the mall experience with special programs and readings. Anybody who goes into malls knows that between 2:00 P.M. and 5:00 P.M. it's dead. You could shoot a cannon off in most malls; there's nobody but a few senior citizens slowly tramping along in their Reeboks. And they could have done some great things in those hours to bring more people in.

Or, they might have emphasized books as great gifts. When you're in a mall, there's a strong likelihood that you're looking for a gift. If it's Father's Day, hang those banners all over the place. Advertise that you have a book on fishing, a book on baseball. Feature it, show it. The consumer would need to know that Waldenbooks is a terrific place for gifts. Promote books as gifts with a gift registry, holiday tie-ins, a lenient returns policy. Offer cards and gift-wrapping. This is what will stick in shoppers' heads. And it's exactly what Amazon.com has done in spades.

The management running the show at the time, however, had no time for it. It was all shot down. They had tried gift-wrapping once, they said, and it had failed. Of course, they had neglected to promote it, so shoppers had no idea the stores offered the services. They could have done all sorts of things if they wanted to commit and spend the money to do it. They had to stand for something. It might have taken a year or two to see results, but eventually that brand would start to pay dividends. They told me they weren't interested.

As so often happens, new management at Waldenbooks finally was brave enough to step out and clearly state what the brand is and who it serves. Waldenbooks is the mall bookstore, serving the needs of mall shoppers, hyping seasonal gift opportunities in a convenient, no-fuss manner.

Defining the Brand

Many companies either forget or deny that they're a brand, then neglect how they're being perceived by consumers. If you don't work at defining yourself, somebody—consumers, the media, your competitors—will.

I was doing a study to help Bergdorf Goodman relaunch their men's store and was meeting with Dawn Mello, the store's president and an icon in the fashion industry. She wanted to make sure I understood that consumers were not going to tell her what was fashion. She knew and her buyers knew. Sometimes they hit and sometimes they didn't, but no shoppers—no matter who they were—were ever going to dictate what fashion was and what they should merchandise. In her eyes, Bergdorf was not a brand, like snack food or detergent.

Her fear was that I would do focus groups and come back and report that customers wanted tiger-striped pants and double stitching on their lapels. Or they wanted Bergdorf's to sell more red V-neck sweaters and fewer cordovan loafers. I told her that my goal was only to understand upscale male customers, how they felt about shopping, and how that might translate into how Bergdorf's could talk to them.

I talked to six groups of men in New York City, all of whom had spent more than $10,000 on clothes in the past year. They were divided between the Bergdorf loyalists and men who were spending the same amount of money in other stores like Saks or Barneys. They weren't necessarily the type of men I expected. I thought they were going to be predominantly gay. They weren't. I thought they would be snooty and snobby. Hardly any of them were. I thought they were all going to be professionals. Maybe half were. Instead, I found a unique group of men who really cared about clothing. They shopped in their own male way, but it was much closer to how a woman shops than the way a man generally does. These men had a lot of money, and they really loved clothes. It was not just status. They liked the way a well-tailored suit fit them. It made them feel better, made them go out and do their job better. If they had free time between business meetings, they were likely to shop at a good store and could spend two or three thousand dollars on a suit.

They were a remarkable group of men, yet a lot of them were absolutely, positively, intimidated by Bergdorf's. They didn't think they belonged. They were afraid they would walk in and be ignored. One man compared it to being the first guest at a party. "The hors d'oeuvres are perfectly laid out and you don't want to touch anything. You even think you shouldn't be there. And your host is sort of annoyed that you are."

On the other side of the aisle, the sales staff I interviewed talked about going out of their way to please the customer. They told of driving out to Kennedy Airport in a blizzard to get a client a suit he needed for a meeting. Anything for the customer.

By not focusing attention on its brand image for fear of being lumped in with supermarkets and malls, Bergdorf's had scared the perfect customer right out of his Guccis. The company considered itself the ultimate resource for discerning men, but it wasn't tending its image. Before the consumer makes up his mind about where and how you fit in his world, tell him your side.

Brands differentiate themselves in the consumer's mind. What are you good at? What do you do better? Stand up for your brand and you have a good chance of convincing the customer you have something of value to offer.

LISTENING POINTS

- ◎ Image isn't everything, but it's a whole lot.
- ◎ Your brand is the sum total of your assets.
- ◎ Be patient. Be consistent. Be focused.
- ◎ If you have no brand image, this is a great opportunity to step forward and stand for something.
- ◎ If you don't tell the consumer what your brand stands for, the consumer may make something up.

9

LASTING BONDS

The Emotional Attachment between Consumers and Brands

It's one thing to establish a brand identity. The next level of achievement is to solidify the relationship so that customers not only know the brand, but relate and believe in it, and are loyal to it through adversity. Your brand must be so deeply ingrained that using another brand just feels wrong. If you always put on your right shoe and then your left shoe, try doing it in the other way around. This discomfort is how loyalists feel when they use another brand.

We buy products because of what they do. We buy brands because of how they make us feel. Brands are about perceptions and impressions. The brands we gravitate to give us reflections of ourselves in our most positive light. That reflection is smiling, inviting, unwavering, loyal, and consistent. Our brand choices speak of confidence, status, entitlement, discernment, and empowerment.

An emotion is involved in almost every choice consumers make in choosing one brand over another in any category. You don't just close your eyes and pick. You want to get a hand lotion, you want to get a car, you want to get a computer—how do you choose? The emotional attachment that develops is related, not to products, but to brands.

Something resonates . . . the brand and the promises made by its advertisements and the look of the packaging: It all suddenly works and it slips into the right slot and what the brand is saying to you feels comfortable. You want what that brand has.

Do you believe a $25 Lancôme lipstick is really that much better than a $5 Maybelline one? Why will a teenage boy only wear a Phat Farm shirt, a teenage girl carry a Kate Spade bag and not the knockoff? Why do you choose Tropicana or Minute Maid? In large measure, we make purchasing decisions based on how we feel about a brand, what we think it says about us, what it represents as a symbol of our self-esteem.

Take toothpaste. I may prefer gels to paste, mint stripe to baking soda white, and probably more than one divorce has transpired over a messy roll of the tube. All that is behavior; it has nothing to do with whether I'm using Crest or Colgate, and it would be the same regardless of the brand. But I *feel* differently toward Crest than I do toward Colgate. When I pick up that tube of Crest, I think *this is recommended by 9 out of 10 dentists* so I'm smarter for using Crest. I grew up with Crest; it feels familiar, homey. I believe in Crest. I want to be associated with this brand.

Go into your local Target or Wal-Mart. Walk down the toothpaste aisle. Five shelves of toothpaste, each six feet long. A world of whitening, brightening, plaque-preventing options. What do you choose and why? Do you nonchalantly pick up any tube and toss it in your basket, saying, "It really doesn't matter because they're all the same," even if that happens to be true?

More and more, our relationship with the brands we prefer goes beyond the quality of the product. Given the overwhelming volume of products and versions of products and slivers of difference among them, in most categories the amount of competition assures that the product will perform as expected. A dependable product has become the price of admission. Forging a bond between the consumer and the brand is what distinguishes one product from the next. When there are multiple brand choices in virtually every product or service category, brand appeal becomes a company's most valuable if intangible asset.

In purely brand terms, there's really no difference in how and why we ultimately prefer a variety of toothpaste or an airline. An airline simply has more moving parts — reservations, service, routes, frequent flyer programs. In the 1980s, United asked passengers to fly the friendly skies, not the best airline, not the one that has the best routes, not the one with the best on-time record. The United strategy pinned its hopes on passengers choosing to fly with them and not another carrier who flies to exactly the same place, based on a belief that, all else being equal, United was the airline that's nicer, more attentive, and more caring than the other guys.

The positioning worked until all else wasn't equal. When other airlines raised the bar on consumer conveniences and schedule accuracy, United didn't keep pace. No one cared about friendly skies when their flight was canceled or when the pilots struck. But if the positioning had been better cemented into a relationship beyond a Gershwin tune, and if it had permeated all the moving parts that make up the brand package, passengers would have stuck by United.

Tylenol succeeded on many fronts when a lethal contaminant found in some of its packages gave rise to the "Tylenol Scare." Aside from the company demonstrating a rarely seen monumental corporate responsibility, the brand had also established itself strongly as the brand of choice by hospitals and families. It had become synonymous with trusted and safe relief to the extent that consumers defended it rather than abandoning it.

To win a following, a brand not only has to have value in its products but a set of values that connect it to the consumer, something more than a list of ingredients or services. Nike is more than the swoosh and its plethora of gear; it stands for active, athletic endeavor. (As of this writing, the brand has become somewhat tarnished and Nike is attempting to polish up its image by addressing concerns about manufacturing in Third World countries.) Disney isn't movies and amusement parks; it's wholesomeness and family entertainment. Woolite might be able to get mud stains out of jeans, but because it stands for delicate, gentle, it will probably never get the chance to prove its grit.

Everything I Know I Learned from Focus Groups

My epiphany came when, early in my career, I was conducting research for Colgate-Palmolive as part of their new products initiative of the early 1980s to expand into different categories. Haircare categories were exploding as higher priced salon brands were starting to make inroads. By then, Vidal Sassoon had long since moved from Great Britain to the local mass merchandiser shelves. Pantene was the premium brand. The era of intense proliferation was in its infancy. Also in its infancy were alternative qualitative research techniques to drill down to the consumer's innermost needs. Our client had concluded that two-hour, one-on-one depth interviews would yield results. Thus we were schlepping a suitcase full of hair-care props and talking about hair care to three women a day for two hours each (even therapists don't take two hours). These labor-intensive and revealing interviews included putting all the shampoo brands on the table and asking the respondent to line them up along a spectrum from best to worst shampoo.

Still new at my job, I was amazed that they didn't rate them in the same order I did. Every interviewee thought the shampoo she used was the best. More amazing to me, they all used the same language to justify their preference: Why is Prell the best? Great lather, really makes my hair feel clean, leaves my hair soft and silky and manageable? Why Sassoon? Same answer. Why Breck? Why Pantene?

So, if all the shampoos performed equally, why were brand preferences so strong? It began to dawn on us that perhaps there was a stronger emotional link to brands than we had considered. We wondered if there was another product category where the decision probably was emotional. We all concluded that automobiles would be a good place to start. After all, Americans have had a virtual love affair with the car since the early days of Ford. Chrysler was the first brand to give Ford a run for his money by taking a chance that people in their dustbusters and goggles might feel differently if the car were a color other than black. It worked. And what else but an emotional response would account for why we might strongly desire a car of another color. So, we asked respondents to think of shampoos as automobiles. Which brand of shampoo was the Cadillac, the Bentley, the VW Bug, the Chevy, the pickup truck, the station wagon? We suddenly got a lot more information. It wasn't so much about how their preferred shampoo made their hair feel as how it made the women feel.

Here's where consistency of response started to emerge. No matter which brand was preferred, respondents agreed that Pantene was the Cadillac. Suave was like the VW bug. Prell was the family station wagon. And so on.

Next, we asked women to tell us how they felt about the car, and here's where brand understanding got even richer. The non-user of Pantene described Cadillac as a car for ostentatious people, whereas the Pantene user felt that the Cadillac was a car that offered great performance and comfort. And another nonuser said that she hoped some day to own a Cadillac.

Aha, shampoo brands can be aspirational. This was a strong emotional consideration that ran like a virus through marketing efforts of the 1980s when yuppies all craved status and emotional branding was born.

For us, that was a magical moment of discovery. We realized that as researchers, we had to introduce new techniques to find out how people felt. We had to move away from the tangible aspects of the product and get closer to the emotional bond the consumer must feel with these brands. Technological advances meant that all manufacturers were developing similarly performing brands at the same time. The functional benefit as a unique selling proposition (USP, coined by Ted Bates in the early days of marketing) was no longer the gold standard. The new flag was an emotional bond and an emotional benefit. Whether shampoos, automobiles, scouring pads, or motels, the emotional bond would be the differentiating factor among the brands.

Emotional Value

Manufacturers would like to think that a brand selection is based on a rationale set of decisions. On many occasions, I've been asked to take consumers through some form of decision tree—to say, what's the first choice that you make among brands, then what, and then what? Hypothetically, the consumer standing at the aisle and thinking about scouring pads, is expected to answer, first it's how dirty my pots and pans are, then it's how big the box is, and finally, it's pricing that determines my decision.

This type of rationale thinking may very well exist in some categories, but it is increasingly being replaced by a quicker, more efficient, simpler, and more meaningful emotional response. Someone looking for a house goes in with all sorts of rational criteria, but most of the purchase is based on emotion. People walk into a house and they think, I'm comfortable here. I can see myself living here. I feel good. It's me. I can relate to it. All of a sudden, their need for a two-car garage disappears because they have fallen in love with the feel of the house; they justify that the existing one-car garage is really all they need, and they buy the house. It's the same thing with brands. At some critical point, it all comes together. Making the right emotional appeal makes the difference.

If you're going to sell anything, first consider its functional benefits and then how that will translate into emotional ones. Focus groups can steer you in directions that will allow you to effectively deliver your message, but consumers aren't mind readers. You can't assume the consumer is going to necessarily figure out your product's benefit without some guidance from you. In doing work for Bayer aspirin, pain relief seemed to be what it was all about. *I ache . . . I take a Bayer . . . I don't ache.* That's the functional benefit but the more important one, the emotional benefit, is how customers feel as a result of not having the pain anymore. Clients new to marketing may think what they should do is come up with a way to advertise that their product is more effective at eliminating pain. Your headache will be gone faster, your headache will be gone sooner, your headache will be gone more completely, your headache will be gone without stomach upset. Those are all functional benefits. Claims like these had their moment in the sun during the early black-and-white days of television advertising.

Today, advertising needs to get at the emotional benefits: Once the pain is gone, you'll be a calmer better mother, your kids won't suffer from your bad moods, you can do that presentation on Monday morning you're worried about, so you'll be a better person: You'll have more *confidence*. I've found that the key emotional benefit that seems to cut across all categories is increased confidence. Lately, I'm noticing more about enhanced lives and that fits well into another big emotional benefit, comfort.

In the 1950s and 1960s consumers liked food compartmentalized in little trays that separated the meat from the potatoes. The functional benefit was an effort-free way to have a hearty three-course meal, including dessert. The emotional benefit: probably, mother's guilt-free satisfaction that her family was still eating a meal.

Now we eat a lot of combined foods, noodles with some vegetables and meat mixed in, a special kind of rice with a prevalent seasoning. With an on-the-go lifestyle, it's easier and quicker to eat a bunch of stuff mixed together. In this world, bowls offer a more functional benefit than compartmentalization. Bowls offer a nice presentation; you can root around and pick what you want without food slopping out, and it's easier to eat on the run holding a bowl.

We started talking about bowls in some work I was doing for one of the big frozen food brands that was wondering about the success of the Uncle Ben's Rice Bowl phenomenon. When you eat from a plate, you don't pick it up and take it to your mouth, but when you're eating from a bowl, it just seems to beg for this maneuver. Eating out of a bowl proved a more intimate experience, something Asians have known about bowls for centuries.

People seem to have an emotional attachment to bowls—you hardly ever read about anthropologists digging up a plate—and the latest round of Uncle Ben's advertising indicates that perhaps they heard the same thing in their focus groups. The new campaign is almost orgiastic as it shows women enjoying Uncle Ben's up close, so the aroma becomes another meaningful benefit of the whole eating-from-a-bowl phenomenon.

There's also something comforting about eating from a bowl, which goes hand in hand with the emergence of comfort food as a gastronomic trend. Although there are those among us who balk at paying premium prices to eat meatloaf and mashed potatoes at the latest impossible-to-score-a-reservation restaurant with a decor like Mom's dream formica kitchen, eating out of a bowl rides along the high curve of that trend.

In the midst of probing the area of bowls, the topic of lids surfaced. The benefits of lids and frozen entree bowls were not immediately obvious. Lids are associated with keeping leftovers fresh, and users said that they rarely had anything left from their container meal. So at first blush, providing a lid seems, well, stupid. That's the likely conclusion consumers would draw if left to their own devices. This is where the marketer has to step in and say, wait a minute, here's why this is such a brilliant idea.

By listening to a few—that's really all it takes—smart consumers, we discovered how lids could turn into an opportunity to differentiate a bowl entrée for my client. Lids became far more appealing when positioned as a way to keep prepared food warm if the meal is interrupted, a common occurrence during lunch at work. Maybe Uncle Ben's doesn't have a lid, maybe your brand does. Every time the consumer thinks of healthy frozen food in a bowl, now it's, "I want that new frozen food entrée that comes in a bowl, the one that's got the lid." But you have to tell consumers, show them at work: *A guy at a desk, eating, eating, eating, phone rings, "Okay, oh gee, I'll get that right out," put the lid back on, clock shows half-hour goes by, that's over, lid comes off, back to eating.*

The marketer defines and positions the benefit. The consumer interprets that benefit from an emotional perspective. This bowl stuff tastes pretty good. Because I'm eating it up close and personal, I also know that it smells great. It's quick, it's easy. I won't spill it on my computer, and eating it won't take too much time away from my job. Eating lunch in a bowl with a lid, therefore, makes me a better and more efficient employee.

Emotions and the Internet

Over the long haul, you have to reach the heart as well as the brain. I recall hearing an Internet advertising agency saying consumers don't care about emotion anymore. It is true that the Internet has contributed greatly in creating more educated consumers. In the privacy of their homes and offices, consumers are able to look at the screen and see that a Panasonic model may be $299.00 and Sony makes a similar product with the same features, and it's only $289.00. Click, I'm getting the Sony.

What the dot.com losers didn't realize is that the consumer-at-screen, like the consumer-at-shelf is bringing a whole bunch of emotions to the party. In the case of televisions, there's probably a Panasonic loyalist who's noticing the price differential and ignoring it: "Panasonic has never let me down. Sony doesn't need my business. I'm going to get Panasonic for only $10.00 more."

Shopping sites also failed to fully understand brand power. If Amazon.com offered the new Michael Crichton book for $29.95 and Barnes & Noble.com priced it 20 percent less, and Discountbooks.com was cheaper than both, the folks at the imaginary Discountbooks.com might well have thought that they had the market in a basket. They would have learned otherwise as Web sites began to develop their own emotional brand identities, coupled with easy navigation (like supermarkets), familiarity (like lodging), customization, and the elusive friendliness.

When I'm buying a book, I feel like I belong at Amazon.com. I feel at home. They seem to know my tastes. It's a friendly shopping experience. Why even waste time at other sites. This was the brilliance of Amazon.com.

Starbucks may be put down by people who see it as the emblem of entitled, young, carefree professionals who are willing to pay $5.00 for a coffee concoction; its customers, however, exhibit an astounding loyalty to the brand, tantamount to worship. Starbucks stands for more than coffee. The brand represents a desired frame of mind. Starbucks sees it as a culture.

You have to do more than just get your name out there. Your brand has to mean something to the consumer. Inventive dot.com advertising pushed the right buttons in building brand awareness, but neglected to push clever Super Bowl advertising into the next level. We may all appreciate the Monster.com "When I grow up I wannabe . . ." commercials, but we need to know how that brand differs from other job sites.

LISTENING POINTS

- ◎ Brand preferences reflect how we see ourselves.
- ◎ Brands create a relationship with your consumer.
- ◎ Most of brand preference is on an emotional level.
- ◎ Translate your brand promise into an emotional payoff.
- ◎ A genuine brand bond is usually price resistant.

10

A BRAND FOR ALL TIMES

The Essence of Loyalty

I drive Saabs. I love Saabs. If you asked me whether you should choose a Volvo or a Saab, I would tell you to get a Saab. Saab's marketing goal should be to continually nurture and reinforce its relationship with me and people like me.

As a loyal customer, I provide two crucial functions. First, I'm your core customer. I will return regularly to purchase your product or service. In fact, I will tend to trust any product that bears your imprimatur. I have faith in what you tell me and then sell me. I would buy a Saab bicycle or motor scooter if Saab decided to market one. Porsche has gone into wristwatches, and why not? Based on what you believe about Porsche, wouldn't you accept the possibility that a Porsche wristwatch would be a skillfully engineered piece of wrist machinery with great style?

Second, as a loyalist I will help sell the brand product for you. I will proselytize for your brand. The people I tell about your brand are more likely to respect and trust my opinion than a multimillion-dollar ad campaign. Loyalty stimulates word-of-mouth, and word-of-mouth cannot be purchased for any amount of money. I've already convinced three of my friends to buy a Saab and all it cost Saab was a $1,500 Loyalty Rebate in 1997.

My convictions about brand loyalty marketing have been influenced by Larry Light, a perceptive marketing consultant whose credo is "brand loyalty is the basis for enduring, profitable growth." He charges marketers to engage in a mutually beneficial dialogue with their customers because loyalty, though invaluable, is also a fragile commodity that needs constant care and surveillance.

Through Larry, I became involved in conducting qualitative research for *The New York Times*. I've been working with them since 1995, closely observing how the newspaper's thinking about their readership has evolved so that today I would choose them as the poster child of great brand-loyalty marketing. Our history together, which as of this writing encompasses interviews with over 1,000 current or potential *New York Times* readers provides an enlightening case study. No other company that I've been associated with has recognized the supreme importance of the loyal consumer and worked harder to foster and maintain that relationship.

Signs of the Times

Prior to my involvement, whenever *The New York Times* executives conducted any kind of qualitative research, they would set up focus groups with broad groups of people who subscribed to the newspaper, balanced by broad groups of theoretically potential readers. And they would go home depressed.

The non-*Times* readers would tell them that the articles were too long, they didn't have the time to read it, they couldn't get through it, they found it just physically too big to read on public transportation, and the paper was intimidating. What they heard from subscribers often wouldn't get their blood pumping faster either. In the mix were those who adored the paper, along with those who only read it sporadically, who subscribed as a status symbol, or who got it simply out of habit.

Light's mantra is cater to the loyalist. Most marketers don't see this as a big enough opportunity. Most marketers want to be all things to all people. They want everybody to know about them, buy them, use them, and yes, even to need them. One of the hardest things to remember is that you're not after the whole world and it's okay that the whole world doesn't need you. Unless you truly are a mass-market brand like Colgate where your market is best defined as "people who have teeth," it's simply foolhardy and ultimately counterproductive to feel that the world is your oyster, or even that most of the world could be your oyster. It's a deadly trap. Even *The New York Times* was falling for the bait by concentrating much of its effort on broadly increasing circulation and thereby ignoring its most devoted readership base.

The paper conducted focus groups because they knew they had to listen to their readers. They never realized that they would learn a lot more if they separated out and listened only to the readers who loved their paper seven days a week, cover-to-cover loved it, couldn't start their day without it. For the first time, *The New York Times* decided it was going to listen to that core group of loyalists whose day didn't dawn if *The New York Times* wasn't at their doorstep.

At first, the editorial people were opposed to this approach because, like Bergdorf's Dawn Mello, they felt that marketing might be tempted to use the input from loyalists to suggest content. They didn't want to entertain the remotest possibility that readers in a focus group who said that they wanted shorter stories or a page of horoscopes every day might get their wish. They were not going to stand by and let anyone breach the firewall between editorial and promotion and marketing.

The huge misconception about qualitative consumer research is that it tells you *how* to do your job. What carefully collected consumer information can do is let you know *if* you're doing your job and possibly provide insights about *why* certain marketing strategies are working or not. Especially in brand loyalty marketing, the consumer isn't a dictator but a collaborator. You should do periodic research with your loyalists to make sure you're communicating the right positioning. You might want to test different advertising approaches or understand up front how best to integrate changes seamlessly. And always you want to find new ways to talk to and reward the loyalty of consumers.

I began with 10 hour-long, in-depth interviews with *The New York Times* faithful. Along with Michael Grissom of *The New York Times* Strategic Research Department, one of the editors attended the first round of depth interviews we did with *Times* diehards in Westport, Connecticut. As the editor listened to readers, he began to realize they weren't telling him how to change the paper. What they were telling him was how much they loved the paper. These were people who couldn't imagine life without the paper. If they had to, they would pay more for it. They made the time to read *The New York Times*, even if doing so meant getting up at 5:30 in the morning just to have that extra half-hour. In contrast to the non-loyalist studies that lined up legions with excuses for not reading the newspaper, the loyalist research revealed a cadre of readers who adjusted their whole schedule to accommodate *The New York Times*.

Afterward, Michael Grissom asked me to do a presentation in two days, hardly sufficient time to prepare. It was a dismal rainy day, I arrived half an hour late, and I found a room full of representatives from the editorial, marketing, promotion, and circulation departments waiting to hear from me. I had never heard such amazingly loyal customers as *The New York Times* readers, and it was crucial to impress this audience with the unique position they were in.

"Do you realize people get up at 5 o'clock in the morning to make sure they read you?" I told them. "One of our respondents had stopped dating a potential husband mainly because he didn't read *The New York Times*."

I had done personal analogy work with *The New York Times* readers and got magnificent, eloquent answers. Some that I've carried around with me:

> "*The New York Times* is like a peony," said a Westport gardener. "That's the traditional Chinese emperor's rose because it's so breathtaking and there's nothing else like it."
>
> "*The New York Times* is like Mark Twain," said a high school English teacher. "He was the quintessential American wit, with a bit of the curmudgeon thrown in. But uniquely American in character."
>
> "*The New York Times* is like a helicopter," said an electrical engineer who chose not to focus on four-wheeled vehicles, "because it doesn't just go up and down. It hovers and gets to know the terrain, then it zeroes in and gets you where you need to be with no effort."

The New York Times is a brand, but it's also a product, and like most products, it offers benefits to its customers. When we discussed the benefits of reading *The New York Times*, it was very consistent, but I had also noticed differences depending on whether we were talking to weekday readers or weekend readers. So, I made up my own analogy to explain the difference. "Your readers seem to be after different benefits depending on whether they're weekly or Sunday only, but what both segments have in common is almost like an addiction to *The New York Times*. The

Sunday reader, you could think of as someone who takes a bath to relax because that's how readers use your paper on the weekend. The weekday reader is more like someone taking a shower to get ready and prepared because that's how those readers use your paper. It's a tool: They use it to get them going." As obvious as it might seem, finally here was someone confirming for them just how incredible consumers thought this newspaper was. Once they realized there was no intention of dumbing down the paper, the editors got excited. My work concerned itself with marketing this brand and this product as is. My job wasn't to tell *The New York Times* to make fewer columns, to put this story on the right-hand side of the page, to make sure they give more coverage to the Bronx or Queens instead of to Manhattan or to write an article in a way that would attract more national readers. All we were doing was talking to readers about the product that the newsroom put out. That product is the brand that instills the loyalty.

They began to see that they had a large nucleus of people who adored anything that *The New York Times* did as long as they continued to be *The New York Times*. Based on that, they wanted to know what to do next.

At the time, *The New York Times* was working on its national expansion program, and was making itself available in not just major cities, but everywhere across the United States. The next logical step, then, was to go out and do depth interviews throughout the country to see if the national edition had the same level of loyalty.

In the meantime, the Strategic Research Department did a major quantitative survey to see if what the depth interviews had proposed about loyalty to *The New York Times* would pan out. It did—statistically, anyway, an enormous and gratifying percentage of all *New York Times* readers may be qualified as loyalists. This was even more exciting news for the newspaper, and marketing, promotion, and circulation revamped their programs to woo and maintain the loyalist.

The quantitative study had isolated several characteristics and correlations about loyal readers. On the one hand, they suggested what these folks were like and how best to reach them and to keep them happy. In addition, the researchers were able to develop a set of characteristics that could be used for locating potential *New York Times* readers with more accuracy than simply sending out a mass mailing. When these characteristics were bundled together, the picture that emerged was of a "like-minded nonreader."

So now, rather than aiming for a moving and largely undifferentiated target, *The New York Times* was able to streamline its marketing and promotional efforts to talk to potential readers and subscribers with the greatest like-minded potential. These prospects were virtually carbon copies of *The New York Times* loyalist, except that they weren't yet reading the newspaper.

In our continuing projects, we always spoke to loyalists and their nonreader counterparts. The tremendous enthusiasm for *The New York Times* continued to manifest itself among loyalists of the national edition. In fact, because people paid a premium for *The New York Times* in areas outside New York City, they were even more devoted to the paper than New Yorkers. When they got the paper, they pored over every page. They might have read the paper two days after breaking news had appeared on TV and still devoured stories that would give context to that news. *The New York Times* fed their curiosity like no other publication.

Moreover, loyalists have such deep respect for the paper that not only do they carry the paper with them throughout the day, they hesitate before heaving it into recycle bins. They leave *The New York Times* for others to read in a doctor's waiting room, around the office, at their morning stop for coffee. That's the thing about loyalists. They want to share the brand, they want other people to know about it. *The New York Times* could advertise endlessly, they could discount subscriptions, they could promote the paper extravagantly, they could get celebrities to talk about it, but they would never be able to capture the value of a reader saying to somebody else, this is a terrific newspaper.

When they got together with Bozell, their advertising agency, to develop a loyalty campaign, the marching orders for the agency: Don't waste a lot of time explaining why people should buy *The New York Times*. A loyalist knows that. Talk to these people. The purpose of this campaign is not to sell more *New York Times* to people that don't read *The New York Times*. It's to say to the loyalists you're reading a great paper. The more you support the loyalist's decision to use your brand, the greater the likelihood he or she is going to continue to be your strongest advocate.

Instead of entreating people to buy *The New York Times*, they came up with the brilliant *Expect the World* campaign, and directed advertising toward the intelligence of the newspaper's reader. Based on the loyalists' love of language, the paper incorporated a series of anagrams into the campaign. In one print ad for the newspaper's popular science section, a herd of look-alike sheep heralding cloning turned "reproduce" into "procedure." Interestingly, when I talked to *New York Times* loyalists in a series of focus groups, they got the word play. When I asked like-minded nonreaders, on the whole, the twist passed them by.

For the paper's devoted, the campaign reinforced exactly what they enjoyed and had come to expect from *The New York Times*. It was clever, witty, cosmopolitan, articulate, provocative, and aroused their insatiable curiosity.

The Times wasn't waving a white flag on increasing readership. What it wanted was a double-barreled effort. First, send flowers to the loyalist. Second, take advantage of knowledge about loyalists to talk to those similarly minded people who aren't yet *Times* readers. The quantitative survey revealed that *The New York Times* loyalists shared a key common trait . . . not affluence, not intellectual bent, but curiosity. This tidbit of information opened up an avenue for approaching the like-minded nonreader.

Invariably, the perception from that nonreader was *too much:* too much New York City, too much news on the political scene, too much international stuff, too much print, too much paper to hold.

In the depth interviews we conducted with this group, we handed out copies of the paper, and watched and questioned them as they read *The New York Times.* As they read it, invariably they would find articles directed at their particular interests. No longer so overwhelmed by the vast scope of coverage, instead they were impressed by how much the paper seemed to speak to their individual concerns. A person from Queens would remark on the reporting on neighborhood stuff. An African American would find a story that put an incident with racial overtones in a political, social, historical context. A computer jock had no idea that *The Times* had a separate section, Circuits, every Thursday that concentrated only on computers and the Internet. A Chinese immigrant would comment about a piece on a Shanghai entrepreneur.

Locally or nationally, when people start to experience *The New York Times*, they're converted. The quality of the paper keeps them over time. My favorite example of this came from a respondent in Miami:

> When I first retired to Miami, I thought that I'd just pick up the *Miami Herald.* I'd been a *Daily News* reader in New York all of my life. You know, you didn't see a lot of *The New York Times* up where I grew up. So, one day I'm waiting at the doctor's office in Miami and I see that there's a *New York Times.* I pick it up and it's got a story about a book that I was just talking to my wife about. Can you beat that? A couple of days later, I pick up another copy, and there's this article talking about a building

that I used to work in. Can you beat that? And this goes on for a few days until I realize that this isn't a coincidence. This is what happens if you read *The New York Times*. You're always going to find something that's relevant to you.

Changing Times

By its very nature, loyalty marketing implies a responsibility. You're saying to the consumer, be my friend and I promise I'll be good to you. Ergo, when you plan to alter what you're doing, the loyalist needs to be informed. You're not asking permission as much as you're maintaining a relationship, saying we'll get through this together. Going to color was one of the paper's most monumental decisions, akin to adding photographs at the turn of the century. Naturally, *The New York Times* was exceedingly concerned about devoted readers' reaction. They wondered if loyalists, who were not a timid bunch, would come at them with broomsticks and lanterns.

Rather than ask readers what they would think if *The New York Times* went to color, we thought a far better test would be to give people a color copy of the paper and see what would happen. We created a prototype from an actual edition, told participants it was an issue from a couple of weeks back, and asked them to show us how they normally read *The Times* and to comment on anything that they wanted to comment on. (This is another example of questions that aren't questions.) Loyalists would pick up the paper, put some sections aside, look at the top right-hand corner of the first section because they knew that's where the top news story was, flip it to check out the below-the-fold story, open the paper up, and remark on the traditional placement of the Cartier and Tiffany ads on pages 2 and 3, thumb through some articles, and continue going through the paper in their usual fashion. Minutes later, I would find myself asking if they noticed anything different about the paper.

Quite a few would look it over and say, "The editorials are still back here. This is a Tuesday paper so here's the Science section." It took a long time before these habitual *Times* readers even noticed the color, despite the prototype's decidedly blue tint.

And when probed, nobody said don't do it. What we did hear were comments like: "*The New York Times* doesn't have to do this. They're the best paper in the world. But I can understand why they want to do it. It will probably attract more younger readers. You don't need it for me. I'll never stop reading the paper. I'll read it no matter what you do. It's sort of nice. Sure, why not."

The clear suggestion from readers was if you're going to do it, do it. Readers trusted that their brand wouldn't turn into *USA Today*. That's another big issue with loyalists—trust. *The New York Times* wanted to be certain they weren't abusing that trust. There were sound business reasons for doing it, but they were very smart to run it by their readers. It gave us the most real-world manner of understanding what might happen. Readers were saying it's a joint effort and, yes, it's okay to do it; and that's what you want from your loyalists.

When the paper was gauging reaction to a putting out a smaller-size paper, again readers didn't particularly care until it dawned on them that articles might be cut. In all marketing, when the package changes, people assume the product has too. As long as readers were assured that content wouldn't be changed or sacrificed, *The Times* could have carte blanche.

Incidentally, *The Times* ultimately decided to stay with its current size. My only caveat for the newspaper was, for every alteration you make, go out and reassure your readership. Take the time to explain what you're doing and why. It goes back to loyalists' curiosity. They want—no need—to know what's going on.

The New York Times doesn't get loyalists' stamp of approval on all its moves. Each time the paper puts in another section, it's changing reading habits. And it raises loyalists' fears that *The Times* will devolve into an unruly mass of syndicated columns and useless sections. But once they realize their apprehension is unfounded and relearning the paper is like renavigating your way around a supermarket after a remodeling, all is usually forgiven.

The New York Times uses the loyalty program in all aspects of its marketing, promotion, and advertising. The Times Card is a device that was well researched prior to making a commitment. Some years back, a company called TransMedia had encouraged *The Times* to offer its TransMedia card to subscribers as a goodwill measure and as a way of encouraging an annual rather than a monthly subscription commitment. If they committed to and paid for 12 months of *The New York Times*, they received a TransMedia card.

This card could be used in various retail establishments (mainly restaurants) to build trade. When buyers showed it, they got discounts that would be reflected back on their credit card statement. A TransMedia competitor had come to *The New York Times* with a similar offer and before renewing contracts, it made sense to see what yearly subscribers, loyalists in the main, had to say.

We learned that the TransMedia card had certain functional drawbacks and that the class of restaurants that accepted it was ever changing and that hardly anybody had really used it when they went out to eat. But what was really interesting was how many people felt it was a disconnect for *The New York Times* to even have such a card. Aside from the fact that *The New York Times* reviews restaurants, there wasn't any other brand tie-in.

This is another powerful dynamic to keep in mind when you've got a brand loyalty promotional effort that you're considering: It has to reflect the brand cachet. Discounts and deals didn't resonate. What subscribers did want was access.

In several different rounds of research, we developed ways of offering access, privilege, and reward to subscribers with the newly christened "Times Card." Today, it's a successful program that fits with the paper's image. Times Card holders can attend monthly events around New York City with their card. They get to hear movie directors, diplomats, famous chefs, best-selling authors, poets, and critics. There are literary luncheons around the country to reward national subscribers.

When we spoke to *Times* loyalists around the country about this program, they noted that in addition to cementing a relationship with the newspaper, attending such events helped them to meet other *Times* readers. Loyalists bond with the brand and usually bond with each other.

With an eye to maintaining and extending the brand, *The New York Times* is constantly trying to come up with programs and initiatives that work in different segments and among different ages. When you go to Starbucks, you see *The New York Times* on sale. This is a great match of two loyalist-dependent brands. In early 2001, *The Times* and the popular and respected TV game show *Jeopardy* formed a partnership.

The paper has developed a curriculum service for high school teachers to use in conjunction with the paper in the classroom. What we discovered is that though many teachers like and use the service, others don't have time to get involved with fact sheets, quizzes, and questions. They use the paper in far more pragmatic ways. A creative writing teacher will show kids *Times* obituaries and say, "This is good writing. Now, using this as an example of a short biography, write one of your own."

They've done research in colleges to try to find out what about the paper resonates with kids on campus and then use that information to encourage a younger generation to read *The New York Times*. To further that effort, they became a sponsor for the annual American Advertising Federation (AAF) competition in which participating business schools develop a marketing plan that will be tested—and if it passes muster—put into practice.

To be done right, loyalty marketing has to incorporate all these bits and pieces. The AAF participation is not going to turn around the newspaper's sales, but it is getting out to the kids who are at the head of their classes in university and college business schools. A lot of these kids never read *The New York Times* until this assignment came around. Now they will carry this experience with them. They will pass on a dedication to *The New York Times*. That's what loyalty is all about.

Loyalist advertising is sometimes criticized as preaching to the converted. But they're also evangelists about their favored brands. Saab sells more cars. *The New York Times* sells more subscriptions.

This same success story could be told for several other brands that I've talked about in focus groups. Starbuck's, Glade Plug-Ins, Lysol, Country Time Lemonade, Tylenol, Altoids, Tropicana Pure Premium Orange Juice, American Express—these are but a handful of brands that have understood the loyalty aspect of marketing and had it pay back over the years.

LISTENING POINTS

- Loyal users sell your brand by generating invaluable word-of-mouth momentum.

- To really understand loyalists, separate them out from the rest of your customers. They should be researched as an affinity group, advertised to as a segment.

- Isolate loyalist characteristics when you're mining for new users.

- Don't confuse having a consumer database with loyalty. The database is just a list. Your loyalists are the soul of your brand.

- Loyalists are codependent with your brand. Don't let them down.

- Check out brand changes or new moves with your loyal franchise. They're like stockholders.

- Loyalty marketing implies a responsibility.

- Brand loyalty has to be earned. This takes time, but the payoff is worth it.

11

BRAND STEWARDSHIP

The Strategies of Winning Brands

Galloping advances in technology may have altered forever the distribution network for goods and services, but they haven't transformed the basic psychology of people. We remain fixated on the same age-old needs and desires. We want the same things, just quicker, instantaneously, yesterday. Word-of-mouth proceeds at sonic speed. And so, the marketing strategies that had holes of *Titanic* proportions—think the demise of Priceline—spell doom that much faster. Online and off, I see promises of how this method or that will serve up a silver platter full of the demographically perfect consumer. Pardon my skepticism, but I see no marketing revolution, only the same mistakes we've always made, now dressed in high-tech garb. With the flameouts of so many dot.coms and e-businesses, maybe marketers will begin to exercise more patience and better control of their brands.

In a world of infinite choice, it doesn't take a genius to know you need to differentiate your brand to build a loyal consumer base. Companies' tactical generals tend to be lured by quick-fix strategies that usually promise far more than they deliver. The consumer is at the end of the road screaming, "Here I am." Careful listening lets you know if you're crawling through an obstacle path to reach them.

Good brand stewardship requires corporate commitment, constant attention, and consistent messages. The strategies that work never forget the core equity of the brand even as the brand grows and stretches its boundaries. The cornerstone of a successful strategy comprises knowledge of a brand's distinguishing characteristics and communication of those differences in a clear, unswerving manner that respects consumer logic and behavior.

What's in a Name

When we hear a brand name, we should have an immediate reference point for how we feel. When the folks at Nabisco began to market their original baby biscuit, they branded it according to how they wanted mothers and their infants to feel: "You need a biscuit" became Uneeda Biscuit.

Today, we go through elaborate computer configurations and hire name specializing companies to help isolate syllables and word bits that, when put together, will form a word that enables emotional bonding. *Accela* is the designation that has been isolated as the preferred name for the new high-speed train that goes from Boston to Washington. I guess it's a soft form of acceleration, but already I've heard consumers in focus groups struggling with the name and wondering if those are hard *c*'s or if they're pronounced like *s*'s. Raymond Loewy had the better idea when he forged ahead with streamlined transportation in the 1920s and 1930s and trains had names like Silver Bullet and 20th Century.

In some work I did with hairdressers on styling products, we were assessing the impact of names on brand bonding. KMS is a professional salon brand whose initials are meant to stand for "Kinetic Molecular System," not a particularly memorable moniker when someone's reaching for that tube from a basket of 20 other options at the styling station.

If you've gone to a chic salon within the past two years, you may have noticed a line of beautifully packaged, vividly colored, and uniquely shaped hair-care products called *Alterna* at the front desk. What I heard from hairdressers was a high recall of the bottles; some even knew that a core benefit of the brand was its hemp ingredient, but the name eluded many. (A few even confused it with the high-speed train.) If the manufacturer wanted our knee-jerk response to be hemp and the benefits it presents, why not use this in the name? What's resulting from this confusion is that the salon professionals are only remembering color and the high price. The name lacks any emotional reference point.

A brand from Tony & Guy is called *Tigi*. When I first saw this product, I pronounced it with a hard *g* as in Tigger from Winnie the Pooh. In focus groups, I learned that it is pronounced with a soft *g* and is shorthand for the initials of the product's originators. Now, they have a sub-brand called *Bedhead*, an evocative name that far outstrips the parent brand in creating an immediate reaction and signaling its intent. Tigi may soon be forgotten but Bedhead has the power to live on.

Brands have emerged from a name, to a symbol, to a code. The best become so entrenched in our daily lives that they enter our language as verbs or adverbs. We *FedEx* our packages, and if you're over 30, you may *Xerox* a document. (Someone was trying to force the issue when they coined, "Do you Yahoo?")

Competition and Brand Integrity

So many clients look at figures and see a competitor running ahead of them, and rather than saying, How can we improve on our performance, keep who we are and what we've got? They forget about their brand and go after what the competition has. This is a quick fix that only looks good on paper. It rarely works and you wind up looking foolish because you forget your own integrity.

In television programming, *Who Wants to Be a Millionaire?* begat *Greed*, *Survivor* begat *Fear Factor*. Which has sewn up the brand identity? Fred Allen, radio wit of days of yore, once said, "Imitation is the sincerest form of television." Another old adage goes, the early bird catches the worm. My response, let him have that worm. There's always another in the ground. If your competitor got there first, find another area in which you can be the leader. Do something that makes you unique, that differentiates you from the other guy and be the first one in that category.

Vodka is America's spirit of choice and super premium vodkas (read: more expensive) rule. Twenty years ago, it was Stoly, then Absolut, now it's Grey Goose and Ketel One with supremacy. It's not a Cosmopolitan, it's a Ketel Cosmo. The au courant drinker perceives a brand like Smirnoff as, "well vodka" which is bartenderspeak for what you get if you don't specify a brand and look like you don't want to spend an extra buck.

A recent distilling client was itching to get past the velvet ropes and join the vodka elite by isolating the right brand image for its own version of a new super premium vodka. As part of the focus groups phase, the liquids guy (that's what they call the person who makes up the spirits) had been told to conduct blind taste tests with Grey Goose versus some formulations that he had concocted to support whatever image finally won the day. I oppose using focus groups to taste test, but the client was insistent, so we arranged a time in the groups when the vodkas could come in, unbranded, to be taste tested, blind, with saltines and spring water between sips.

The groups were surprisingly negative about front-runner Grey Goose. They said it smelled like gasoline and tasted like rubbing alcohol. It won the, "well vodka" classification. In contrast, my client's products received accolades of "smooth," "easy going down," "would make a great martini," and "pleasing aftertaste."

Though my client received very positive feedback, I'm not going to tell him to market his vodka because it did better than Grey Goose. If we had labeled and branded the vodkas, Grey Goose would have been the clear winner. In this instance, people are buying the sizzle not the steak. The A-list territory is claimed, and though this may not be vodka drinkers' final answer, why try to nudge your way into an overcrowded competitive environment? Why try to be like all the others? One positioning in this study was a real winner, but only because it was a truly unique product idea. It gave super premium a new formulation twist and was nudging the curiosity of super premium vodka drinkers, as well as the gatekeeper bartenders who decree which new brands get pushed and which stay in the bottle. All the rest—carefully worded to justify a super premium bar call—were dismissed as clones, and the distiller chided for his lack of imagination in thinking that the trendy bar crowd would clamor for an imitator.

The pattern is familiar. The first brand in gets a boost because the product or its benefit becomes closely identified with the category. He owns the category until proliferation blurs the differences and consumers jump to whatever is momentarily hot. And then, as more brands enter the fray, the battlefront changes and brand managers now confront consumer indifference, or worse, frustration. It happens in vodka, it happened in mints, and it even happened in air fresheners.

The sweet smell of success greeted Air Wick years ago when it came out with Stick-Ups, an air freshening device (research indicated that deodorizing was vile and nasty but freshening was positive and inviting) shaped like a plastic hockey puck and containing a thin disk of cardboard impregnated with fragrance. You were supposed to "stick" it "up" wherever there was an offending odor—by the garbage, the cat litter, the diaper pail, under the kitchen sink. Stick-Ups were Air Wick's attempt to move out of the bathroom and protect the rest of the home.

Air Wick got fragrance happy. If research indicated baby powder was becoming popular, Air Wick introduced a freshener that smelled like a newly bathed infant. When they discovered we liked potpourri, they decided potpourri was a fragrance not a bunch of dried herbs, leaves, and flowers.

Glade, Air Wick's competitor in providing air freshening for the masses, wanted some of the action. As consumers became wary of aerosols, both companies came out with liquids and gels in ever more colorful contraptions. Glade hit pay dirt when they stumbled on the singular idea of reconfiguring their gel product so that you could plug it into an electrical outlet and the heat from the outlet would result in continuous air freshening. They called it *Plug-Ins*. This time, Glade was first off the mark; they had created and owned a whole new category.

But what if you didn't want to smell the roses all the time? Air Wick countered with a product called *AirWaves* that had a switch. Alas, it was twice the size of Plug-Ins at twice the price. They had made a crucial miscalculation. In follow-up focus groups, consumers told us that if they wanted to control Plug-Ins, they unplugged them. The small size of the units was the big draw. They didn't want to pay a penny extra either. Air Wick waved good-bye to its offspring.

Meanwhile, Glade was putting the pedal to the metal and spinning out new Plug-Ins. They had ones that looked like tulips or hearts. They came in multiple colors and patterns. They had holiday collections with Santas and Easter eggs. Then they introduced a line extension—Clip Ons—that had nothing to do with electricity, but you could attach them to places like the visor on your car. Gone was the smell of golden retriever in your SUV.

Still anxious to discover what the next new device was going to be so that they could pull ahead of Glade, Air Wick contracted me to do an ethnographic study. Out in the field we went to examine how America uses house deodorants.

We paid attention to how the house looked and, of course smelled, from the outside to the inside. We took special notice of pets, high on the odorous list. We visited households with lots of children, also up there in smell production. If there were any air fresheners or deodorizers, or whatever they were being called by the respondent, where were they? We started out going to homes that had air fresheners so if there were any plug-in gaps, Air Wick could fill them. Then we went to people who didn't use them but were potential users—people who said they occasionally noticed offensive odors that they would like to eliminate.

First, we learned that usage was elusive. People had air freshening devices sprinkled around their homes, but it was more than likely that they had been buried there for years. Stick-Ups were permanently stuck on. The liquids and gels in their colorful plastic containers had become part of the décor. People had grown accustomed to cleaning around them as they scrubbed behind the toilet, tidied up the litter box or vacuumed out the closet. In fact, while they thought of themselves as good customers, the years-old manufacturing dates on their units said otherwise. They certainly weren't current users. Consumers had them hidden: behind picture frames, under chairs, and within the fold of the family pet's favorite sleeping cushion.

More significantly, the competition was more than Glade and similar foes. We were fighting for a share of the nose with fresh flowers, open windows, baking soda in the kitty litter, fabric soft-ener sheets in the linen closet, scented candles everywhere, and our old friend potpourri. The world was divided between people who adored fragrance and went to any extreme to bring scents into their environment and those who shunned fragrance like a vam-pire avoids the cross. The fragrance fanatics used anything and had everything. They were willing purchasers for anyone who claimed the fragrance battleground across all categories, from pot-pourri to candles to lightbulb rings to drawer paper.

Our key recommendation to Air Wick: Leave Glade their plug connection. Develop potpourri—not potpourri fragrance—along with its accessories and brand it. Move into a whole new area of candles, sachets, and the like. Don't put the products in the cate-gory of deodorizing. Think of them as home enhancement be-cause that's what the pro-fragrance person is seeking. She wants pleasing smells in her home, not just a cover-up for the stench of steamed broccoli.

That was almost a decade ago and consumers are buying more scented candles than ever, whether votives from Glade or hand-dipped ones from upscale home stores like Pottery Barn. Aro-matherapy no longer conjures up visions of scented shrinks' couches and pricey spas. Potpourri may be gathering dust in ev-eryone's bathroom but aromatic products continue to smell very green. Glade moved boldly. The company cornered the market in branded scented products and me-too Air Wick disappeared.

One more note on the competitive marketplace. Just as my client Air Wick had blinders on and could only see a rival in Glade, it's a mistake to look only at the guy running next to you as your competitor. The universe is big and the wider view might open up a world of possibilities or narrow them down to the ones that have real promise.

Recently, I bought a tube of cream to shave my legs from Kiss My Face. It says it's especially for women; it's moisturizing, and it has aloe and some styptic ingredient to stop the bleeding should I nick myself. They have this minuscule market, but their competitive frame is much bigger than they realize. They probably think they're vying solely with soap and shaving cream. They're actually competing with waxing, with using nothing to aid the process of shaving your legs, and with not shaving them at all.

Most clients don't consider the total competitive world for their product or service. Instead of broadening their scope, they just think about "Who else is like me and how can I be better than that other brand?" They'd be far better off asking, "Who else offers my benefits and what do I have to do to convince the consumer to use me?" It took companies that make entrées like Stouffer's a long time to realize that they weren't just competing with other frozen food entrées. The world wasn't made up of consumers wondering whether to buy Stouffer's, Swanson, Lean Cuisine, or Healthy Choice. The choices are wider. Am I going to nuke a meal or am I going to open up a can? Am I going to go out? Am I going to fix nothing? Am I just going to get by on snacks? The competitive realm stretches across a wider range of possibilities.

The broader message here is that to build brand loyalty, companies have to define their points of differentiation within the competitive arena and communicate those qualities to potential customers in an unwavering manner. Consumers expect brands to be true to themselves.

Extending a Brand

Companies prefer to build off of their existing equity, because it's so expensive to establish a new brand. They want to stretch their space on the shelf and limit access for their competitors. There used to be a gentleman's agreement to guard against these turf wars. A tacit arrangement between Procter & Gamble and Clorox assured that Tide would never step into bleach territory and Clorox would never make a detergent, but now it's all fair game. Forget playing nice. Not long ago, I did detergent work and all consumers could talk about was the great new Tide with Bleach Alternative. To gain advantage, to lengthen the reach of the brand, companies try to capitalize on the value of their name, image, status, and relationship with consumers through line extensions into new categories. In previous chapters, I've railed against the rampant product proliferation and concomitant consumer confusion that results from this strategy. But line extension can squander a brand's power in another way.

Companies constantly miscalculate how well their brand's equity will translate into hitherto untrodden areas. Think about this is in terms of a bull's-eye target. The center area is where you have a fit so perfect that consumers assume you already make the product. Coach is known for its fine leather handbags. Before the company put out a line of shoes, customers would have sworn that the luggage leather pumps they bought were from Coach.

Years ago, an old friend of mine had been in charge of new product development at Colgate. He won the great new product award by marketing Colgate Toothbrushes. He got the idea when surveys revealed that almost one out of two consumers said that they were using a Colgate brand toothbrush, and at the time, Colgate was not yet in the market with a toothbrush. This was a no-brainer, and right in the next circle of brand extension work.

Each succeeding circle, however, can put you farther away from your core identity in consumers' minds. I've conducted several studies for Maybelline cosmetics about how far they could extend their turf. The cosmetics world is divided into mass and class and Maybelline is forever on the lookout for ways of getting off the wall in discount stores and onto the floor of department stores.

There is some price point that you can't go beyond with the name Maybelline because its reputation is affordable value. Since the company puts out a well-regarded mascara, it could comfortably meander into a well-priced eye gel. When we pushed the boundaries out to an upscale skin-care line with impressive sounding sea-based ingredients under the Maybelline imprimatur, women told us, "Get outta here, that doesn't work." The apparent inelasticity of the Maybelline brand imagery narrowed the possibilities. The rubber band snapped back. You can imagine what happened when Maybelline tested the waters for umbrellas and pantyhose. Then again, Hanes wouldn't work for a facial moisturizer either.

When Ovaltine wanted to line-extend, nutritional bars came up as a great fit. An Ovaltine snack bar would be in sync with the original product. Line extensions work best when you change the form of your product and maintain the benefit, or keep the form, but substitute another related benefit. Ovaltine in a powder to Ovaltine in a bar, for example, isn't a big leap. It's young, it's energy, it's sort of chocolate malty, yet it's extending out because it's not just another flavor of the powder.

A chocolate drink that also provides protein would be another simple move for the brand. But in this hypothetical case, the nutritional bar segment makes the most sense because the category leader, Power Bar, is almost exclusively tied in with athletes and energy. This could have left a gap for Ovaltine to step into—children, moms, nutrition, chocolate—that would differentiate it from the brand leader.

Then, after they had solidified that position, Ovaltine could have moved into other areas like sports because they'd begun with nutrition and families. Businesses that try to leapfrog the intermediary step risk consequences beyond consumer indifference. Starbucks was going to sell home furnishings on the Internet, and the stock market said no you won't. The stock lost nearly half of its value.

Bayer has taken its brand name into lawn care. Bayer is a huge company in Germany, probably like Du Pont is in the United States, and they're dabbling in a lot of different things. They don't just make little round pills. But for the American consumer, Bayer went from analgesics to the next circle, chemicals, then went out one circle more and came up with weed killer. Nevertheless, every time I see Bayer weed killer, my stomach wrenches a little bit. Somehow, it just doesn't feel right.

On the other hand, Cheerios has done a brilliant job at managing where the brand goes with its name and its little round Os. It's a cereal that adults and kids agree on. Multiple generations have grown up with it, so it transcends age. It has a healthy, oat, not-drowning-in-sugar, reputation. Parents don't worry about the product getting lodged in a child's throat because it melts, and as a bonus Cheerios vacuum up fairly easily. Children love it because of the O. They can eat one at a time and not be too messy.

As they began to look for ways to reach out, Cheerios started with the understanding that they rule in cereal and kids and Os. They came out with Honey Coated Cheerios, which is perfect. Honey is still healthy so it fits in with the Cheerios image. It adds a little more sweetness to the brand but it's not refined sugar; they didn't call it Sugar Frosted Cheerios. They didn't go to the other extreme and turn Cheerios into Grape Nuts. They didn't change the shape or talk about the goodness of Cheerios in your psychic life.

I'm sure there's a mantra repeated back at General Mills that goes, "Kids love us, moms appreciate us, we provide wholesome fun." To line-extend in any way that doesn't respect those equities would have gotten them into trouble and they never did it. Cheerios maintained its dignity and integrity by thinking in terms of an O culture. They introduced little novelty items, like an O purse cum snack holder and a Cheerios book for toddlers. Moms think this is just fine, even though they are reading to their children about a brand and not about a little bear, because Cheerios has built up a history of trust.

The other great circle brand—Life Savers—has worked along the same lines. I had become the darling of Life Savers because I had accurately predicted—with wisdom gained from 6- to 12-year-old boys and girls—that Gumzilla wasn't nearly as good a name as Bubble Yum for a new soft and juicy bubble gum. Mini-mints had become the next new thing and the traditional Life Saver Pep-O-Mints heard the tiny feet of Tic Tac at its heels. (The project's code name was BITE, not because the mints went into your mouth, but to signify the competition biting at Life Savers' territory.)

We were set to do several focus groups to investigate size and shape with teenagers in Connecticut. This being midwinter, Mother Nature had other plans. A huge blizzard left Fairfield County glistening like Austrian crystal. Most businesses had closed because power lines had fallen under the weight of the ice. But since all the R&D and marketing people were there, the kids were off from school, and we had a modicum of heat in our Darien office, we proceeded.

For an entire day, groups of teens huddled in circles as we passed around tiny mint prototypes trying to discern if round was better than oblong, if sharp edges were acceptable and how small was too small. We eventually lost our power too, but we soldiered on until it became impossible to pass around tiny mints to mittened palms by candlelight.

Life Savers never came out with their own version of Tic Tac but what they finally did was hold tight to their own equity, the circle. This realization gave birth to Breath Savers, shaped like

Pep-O-Mints but with the hole filled in with a blue substance that ostensibly freshens breath.

The Arm & Hammer folks transformed themselves from powder in a tired little yellow box that people who baked had on their shelf for 10 years to a ubiquitous household product. When expansionist-minded corporate executives examined the characteristics of the brand, they realized it had a natural de-odorizing component. They didn't have to change the product. They just had to advertise it and tell consumers it was good for the refrigerator. Arm & Hammer began to own deodorizing. Through owning deodorizing, freshening, and natural, they graduated into toothpaste and underarm deodorants, yet they never moved beyond what they essentially were. They went into laundry powder, not a liquid, which wouldn't fit with the brand's primary attribute. Powder was what was in the little box and to ensure consumers got the connection between the stuff in their refrigerator and on their laundry shelf, the packaging design and color remained consistent. The shorter the leap of faith between product extensions, the more likely the consumer will be to make the jump.

Brand Alliances

A winning strategy protects brand essence throughout an organi-zation. Ensuring a consistent message and living up to the trust placed in you by consumers takes corporate commitment to brand-appropriate business decisions. If consumer loyalty is based on an emotional bond, companies must pay strict attention to the intangible aspects of their brands.

A company like Disney closely monitors its image of whole-some fun and family entertainment. Every single thing Disney does has to fit into that identity. The Disney family of brands can never be associated with anything that detracts from that or could disappoint consumer expectations. When they went into the cruise line business, Disney chose to emphasize family-oriented pleasure over the singles' scenes or senior outings. The advertising plays down where the boat is bound in favor of the family experience on board.

American Express has been equally diligent in guarding its brand. Its original alliance with Delta was a brilliant move. When brands form alliances like this, each partner brings along its emotional baggage. Alliances work best when the prestige value of each brand is of similar weight and the brands appeal to the same attitudinal group of consumers.

The first generation of brand alliances or cobranding was promulgated on the concept "buy me because you buy them." The next incarnation moved to "buy me because you like them." In today's alliance marketing, it's "buy me because you trust them." Not only are we looking for brands that we want to hang out with, we expect the brands hanging out with each other to make sense too.

Brand marriages can parlay individual strengths, working to the mutual advantage of both, as in the case of American Express and Delta. In the rush to gain online credibility, many time-tested companies plunged into deals with embryonic dot.coms, only to risk their own good name with consumers when Internet partners couldn't fulfill their half of the bargain. For example, cereal giant Kellogg took a hit after teaming with the ill-fated Toysmart.com.

The New York Times thought long and hard before it formed an alliance with Starbucks. The mega-coffee bar was equally cautious about the proposition of only carrying *The New York Times* in its stores. In fact, Starbucks surveyed its employees and when they all agreed that *The New York Times* seemed a far better match than *USA Today*, the deal was struck. Sales of *The New York Times* have soared.

Price Deferential

Price is a fickle mistress. Lower your price and you certainly might gain converts. But it's a game plan that ignores consumer aspirations. The targeted customer may currently drive a Chevy Malibu but what he'd like is a BMW 325i.

Sometime in the late 1980s, Wal-Mart designated itself as the place to go for everyday low pricing or as it came to be known EDLP. No matter what the day or the week, or which coupons customers remembered to redeem, their brand positioning was that they were committed to having the fairest prices everyday.

Then Procter & Gamble announced that they were going to eliminate traditional promotional efforts, which consumers know as coupons or specials. Other marketers being the trend followers that they are, all decided that lower price, no matter what the category, was what was going to finally differentiate brands in the consumers' minds and ultimately improve their bottom line. After P&G moved on EDLP, everyone else followed suit. In marketing magazines and business books, 9 out of 10 articles were mentioning EDLP as the wave of the future.

If you're selling 50 bottles of analgesics for $3.49, and you can sell 100 bottles for $2.99, you're probably going to be ahead of the game, and the mass retailers love you because your product is moving off the shelf. But if you only appeal to buyers based on price, they won't necessarily care anymore whether they're buying Advil or Motrin or Nuprin (as mentioned, they're very confused by the crowded and cluttered shelves anyway).

I never bought into it. I still don't. I remember warning Colgate toothpaste that pricing was not going to snag them a long-term advantage over Crest. And that's the operative phrase, long-term. Consumers will buy the lowest price, but your brand will soon be reduced to that lowest stature of commodity. You may win for the month or the quarter, but eventually your brand begins to lose its cachet. Hand in hand with positionings like these goes the consumer's assumptions that she's not playing in the big leagues. If you tell the consumer you are the low-price option, she assumes there's a higher priced one. This, then becomes the aspirational brand and anchors the category.

Being perceived as an inexpensive alternative is another story. Lower prices are best used as tiebreakers among distributors. It's fine for Wal-Mart versus Rite Aid. It should not be used as the tiebreaker among brands. Put another way, maybe I'll purchase analgesics from Wal-Mart because I know I can get Bayer cheaper than at the local pharmacy. It's unlikely that most consumers will purchase Bufferin rather than Bayer for a price deal.

In focus groups I did for Bayer around this time, I heard the predictable party line about buying aspirin by price. Here's the array of typical consumerspeak that existed on the surface of my initial question, "Why do you buy the brand of aspirin that you do?"

"I look for the best price. All aspirin is the same."

"I buy depending on the coupon I have with me. All aspirin is the same."

My next question: "Okay, what do you do when you have a coupon for Bayer and Bufferin is the same price?"

"Of course, I would buy Bayer."

My next question: "Why would you buy Bayer if all brands are the same?"

The next answer, and the meaningful piece of consumer learning that can be developed into an insight: "I don't know. I guess it's because Bayer has been around for a long time and it's always stood for quality and I trust it and maybe if there is any difference between brands, Bayer may be just a little better. Maybe it has less fillers. Doesn't it have something to do with reducing the risk of heart attacks?"

My reaction: This is the mother lode.

Also keep in mind, focus groups have more to do with language than with numbers. So even though this comment came from a single panelist, to me, it's extremely valuable. It begins to educate my hunches, and it should set my client's inner marketing wheels in motion thinking about what can be done to reinforce those beliefs. I may follow up with "anyone else feel that way?" or "anyone feel differently?" Invariably, there is a polar opposite panelist in the group who will answer from this perspective: "If all brands cost the same? Well, then it's a matter of whatever my hand happens to grab on that day." I believe this behavior just as ardently as I believe that consumers do differentiate between brands on dimensions other than price.

If customers keep saying you're so expensive, it doesn't mean you have to lower your price. It may mean you're perceived as a premium brand and you have to stand up to it. Never apologize for being expensive. Bergdorf's never cut its price. People who say it's so expensive probably aren't your market . . . yet.

La Prairie makes an extraordinarily expensive skin-care line and it inspires extraordinary loyalty among its users. There's a story, perhaps apocryphal, that Donnatella Versace once said if there was a fire, the first thing she would take is her La Prairie.

In one of the groups I conducted for the company to test out advertising, one woman recalled that when one of her La Prairie products fell, she threw herself on the floor and rolled in the precious oil so she wouldn't waste it.

Ergo, having talked to La Prairie loyalists I knew how staunchly they defended the product. They didn't want to see models and spokespeople in the ads because as they told me, "We are the La Prairie woman. We don't need anybody else to be her. The product is the spokeswoman." You couldn't pay creative to come up with that.

In the late 1990s, the Swiss-based company was embarking on a global non-user initiative, trying to figure out how they could get more women to use La Prairie. Our recruiting efforts were targeted at women aware of La Prairie but users of equally premium-priced skin-care products. We listened to these women talk about their impressions, their perceptions, and their attitude toward La Prairie versus the other costly brands that they used. This wasn't the Maybelline gal; we're talking Sisley, La Mer, and other $100-a-pop-teeny-jar brands.

Within the groups of aware non-users were those who looked at the proposed slick silver-toned ads and said things like "Geez, this stuff probably costs a fortune, I wouldn't touch it with a 10-foot pole" or "It depends on the value of the gift with purchase that they're offering" or "Why should I pay more for a name; it's all the same."

The CEO of La Prairie sat back behind the mirror and said, "Maybe we don't want that customer. Maybe we should just sell more product to the people who love us," which is a perfectly valid conclusion. She didn't huff and pout and say I hate these non-users, a common response. She respected that what they were saying made sense, and as she listened, she realized it was going to be very hard from a business perspective to win them. Her decision was to find another way.

We had observed among some of our aware non-users attitudes similar to those expressed by La Prairie loyalists. The like-minded non-users usually approved of the model-less ads, were extremely loyal to their chosen brand of skin care, religiously followed a skin-care regimen, and were earning comparable salaries. This was the low-hanging fruit that La Prairie could work on and win over.

Sure this approach narrows the customer you're going after but you don't want to alienate that body of consumers who are your bread and butter. If you say the right stuff about yourself, they will find you. Someone asked, "Yeah, but how do we go out and get them?" You don't have to go out and get them, you just have do a good job of being who you are; they'll find you. If you have the right advertising to communicate who you are (and we learned in our studies what the right advertising would be), it will attract the new La Prairie woman. I might be using Sisley, and I might love my counter girl, but if La Prairie finds the right way to talk to me, I'll check out La Prairie.

That's an interestingly different perspective for marketers to have in this day and age, because the feeling among marketers has always been *I want you, I'm advertising to you, I'm targeting you, and I'm going to get you.* My thinking is *I understand you, I think you will relate to me in this way, I think I have a product that you will need and enjoy and I'm going to manifest that in my ads or my computer banner, or my packaging. I know you'll find me, because I'm making an effort to be heard.*

For La Prairie, their advertising communicated upscale, high price, exclusivity, no expense spared to bring you the best. They are talking to the person who will say, "This must be good stuff because I really get the feeling it costs a lot. I'm going to check this out the next time." That was careful listening on La Prairie's part. They had never considered their line in quite that light but they were willing to reevaluate.

As much as I advocate consumer listening, I believe marketers can develop monsters with specials and bonuses. They're simply more trouble than they're worth, and they undercut the intrinsic value of the product. In the beginning, frequent flyer reward programs seemed like a great thing. Now everybody offers points so nobody cares about any of it anymore. Can we really expect the consumer to be any different? Whether I fly United, American, Delta, or Continental, they are all going to give me deals. So the reward has lost its impact.

The credit card people have gone overboard offering credit cards at 4.9 percent that at some mysterious time go up to 18.9 percent. It's always something point 9 percent, so they don't go up to the next digit. The consumer hates those mailings, not to mention the incessant phone solicitations. The only people who show any interest are the indigent, the credit-unworthy, and the ones who are playing the game of perpetually transferring debts from card to card. The credit card companies are not getting the financial slam dunks they thought they would with these offerings.

Teach your consumers to value your brand and then toss in a deal like lower pricing as an occasional bone. Price and special discounts rarely help you go the distance. They don't make your brand stand out, they don't make it unique, and your competition can slash prices or undercut your discount, rewards program, or APR in the blink of an eye.

Say It Again, Say It Again

I was fascinated by an episode of *The West Wing* in which a poll was taken after everybody's favorite president—Jeb Bartlett—had delivered his State of the Union address. He had taken a controversial stance on an issue, perhaps gun control, and his minions were anxious to know how it played in a few key congressional districts. The numbers indicated that he had not gained many new supporters. A top aide took it as a sign they shouldn't go forward with the policy. The woman in charge of conducting the poll vehemently disagreed. Her view: Ratchet it up. Your message isn't getting through, which doesn't mean it's a bad idea or that you won't have a breakthrough. Give it time.

I couldn't have written a better script to plead my case. Impatience is the leading cause of death among great ideas. I did work for Volvo over two decades ago as it was trying to switch its image from solid, boxy, safe, to suave and sexy. That effort is only beginning to pay off. To make an impact, you have to say the same thing consistently over and over again.

It takes about 18 months from the birth of an idea to seeing it on the shelf to consumer awareness. It's like an elephant's gestation period. But manufacturers live and breathe these brands and these products and they have a hard time waiting. The commercial is on the air for a couple of months, and they immediately want to do a focus group. Here's a conversation I have all the time: "We'd like to do some focus groups on our new product, just to see how our target audience is feeling about it, and to make sure that they understand our message."

"How long has the product been out?"

"Since January" (this is in April).

"Did you advertise it?"

"Oh yes."

"Okay, so you want to talk to people who are using your product, and aware of the advertising, and you feel that we'll have no trouble finding them?"

"No."

Well, guess what. We made 2,000 phone calls and found one woman who remembered their ad but didn't know who it was for.

Marketers probably don't set out to change opinion; they set out to sell their product or their brand and learn through research how the consumer feels about them. They want the consumer to feel differently about them. So they change the brand cosmetically—new logo, new packaging, new name—and then they keep testing along the way to see how far they can walk from that image. If Campbell's soup is red but every time the consumer sees that red container they think of old-fashioned imagery and can never imagine Campbell's soup could be lean and mean, marketers probably have to keep some of the red in there. You don't want to walk too far away. There can be an evolution. You can't say something different about your brand and expect the consumer to catch up with you quickly.

The Internet has narrowed the gap, but don't expect instant gratification. Companies think that because they've worked so hard on their commercial, everybody who sees it on television is going to notice it, remember it, and make the connection. Think again. It rarely happens.

The Advantage of Real Consumer Behavior

Companies miss out on significant opportunities when they refuse to listen to and take advantage of real-life consumer usage. Buyers are offering a helping hand. Stop fretting that their ideas for using a product aren't in lockstep with how you conceived, marketed, and advertised it.

Over the years, I've done a fair amount of work with French's French Fried Onions. (Ten years ago, it used to be Durkee's. This is another case where the consumer hasn't caught up and still thinks it is.) They're trotted out by just about every Thanksgiving-celebrating household once a year for that wonderful family favorite "green bean casserole." For the uninitiated, when you make the green bean casserole, you add some french fried onions to the sauce, sprinkle the rest on top, stick it in the oven, and voilá. And everybody admits that those onions are really what makes it. Though the product was introduced as a snack food, nowadays few think about canned fried onions until it is turkey time.

I began one group by passing the can around to have the panel look at the packaging. The first woman said, "Can we open it?" "Sure." No one could keep their paws out of the can. Everybody said, "I always buy more than I need because I know I'm going to eat some, my daughter is going to eat some, my son-in-law can't keep his hands out of it." All I wanted them to do was look at the package, but I watched the way they dove in with gusto.

Egged on by that consumer reaction, I kept urging French's to look for ways to reinforce noncasserole use for their taste treats. People loved the product, yet French's was losing the opportunity to capitalize on that and broaden its scope. After one study, I suggested, "Next Thanksgiving, sell it three for some price and push consumers to stockpile. Don't just have them buy one can, do a deal. Let them know they can use one can for the holiday and one for munching. You could say, here's French's original casserole size and snack size. Join them up at the hip for Thanksgiving."

Something else I liked about this study is that we did it two weeks after Thanksgiving and timing can be critical. You don't want to talk about suntan products in Chicago in February. You want to get things that are as fresh and up-front as possible. Turkey and fixin's were still on their minds, yet shoppers had no clear recollection about how much they had paid for the product. When you're putting together a holiday meal, the price of ingredients really goes out the window. Time-pressured consumers run up and down that aisle, grabbing whatever they need.

As we listened to women talk, there was this high emotional edge about not tampering with the green bean casserole recipe because their families wanted it exactly the same way—they waited all year for it. So the fact that the competitor—usually a store brand—is cheaper shouldn't worry French's. All it has to do is remind consumers of its presence. *Everybody in your family will know it's authentic because you've used French's.*

I'm never sure what finally tips the scales in favor of an idea, but French's recently launched a new campaign for its fried onion rings to emphasize the snacking aspects of the crispy onion treats. If I were French's, I'd give a share of credit for learning about the broader possibilities for the brand to consumers.

In the real world, consumers discovered that Avon's Skin-So-Soft, a highly fragranced bath oil, repelled insects. The word spread like wildfire, but for years, Avon eschewed any effort to promote the bath oil in this manner. Bugs and bathtubs are not a marketing match made in heaven for a personal care toiletries company.

There are, however, other ways to take advantage of unexpected consumer behavior and still sell product. Now, Skin-So-Soft is in hardware stores, side by side with other hardware-counter impulse items like Tweezerman and Hide-A-Key . . . or next to the citronella candles on the shelf . . . or in the seasonal aisle with the Weber BBQ tools. Who cares that women aren't soaking in it?

The Skin-So-Soft fragrance that now pervades outdoor gatherings tells me that Avon's batting a thousand by not restricting its distribution to catalogs and Avon representatives. Do you know who your Avon rep is or how to get in touch with one if you want to buy Skin-So-Soft for the next family picnic? In comparison, how often are you in a hardware store these days?

In most cases, consumers follow the rules. They think about and use products as intended. Why and when they don't can be instructive. The suggestion to think outside the box can often be helped by talking to someone actually outside the box, who may not approach a product with preconceived ideas. Adding consumer input to the strategic mix may jump-start your thinking in new directions.

LISTENING POINTS

- All that glitters is not marketing gold.
- Don't substitute imitation for innovation.
- Line-extend from your own unique position of strength.
- A loyalist will trust your name and reputation on new products.
- Justify your price before you lower it.
- Teach your consumers to value your brand.
- Use pricing, discounts, and rewards only as an occasional bonus.

12

OUTSIDE PRESSURES

Protecting Brands in a Changing Marketplace

On December 12, 2000, General Motors announced that the Oldsmobile would be put to rest after a brand existence of 103 years. Once the symbol of middle-class luxury, the car had outlived its reputation along with its profitability. GM decided to ditch the worn-out model and sink the money into its brands with less history but brighter futures.

Categories and consumers don't stand still, neither can brands. If they don't evolve according to the times, the competitive environment, and consumer need (and sometimes whim), they, like the Olds 88, risk irrelevancy.

Satchel Paige's advice about not looking back because something might be gaining on you remains equally true today. Brands are being developed, finding niches, and becoming objects of affection faster than ever before. Powerful brands require constant vigilance. Without warning, someone could be encroaching on the territory. You may notice a slip in sales this year versus last year, but haven't a clue where the assault is coming from.

Signals of brand changes in the making frequently surface in focus groups, though sometimes it's hard to pinpoint exactly what's going on. Perhaps the dark-horse brand name begins cropping up more often or the faint whiff of dissatisfaction arises at the mention of the front-runner. In doing work for FedEx in the mid-1980s, you could feel the onslaught of drab brown uniforms as UPS made its move on the leading overnight shipper. FedEx was listening with both ears and despite great efforts by UPS, has managed to hang on to its leadership position. Have you ordered anything recently when FedEx hasn't been prominently offered as a shipping expediency option?

Consider the capricious cycle of the restaurant business. You open a restaurant and it's new, it's fresh, and you get the crème de la crème of clientele. It attracts the circle of people who set the trends. Two years later, you reach another plateau and those trendsetters have moved on to the next restaurant, and what you're getting are the friends of those people, who have finally heard about it and now are making reservations. At the last level, you want to sell the restaurant because your customer base has shifted to the parents of the friends of the original trendsetters. (A limousine driver who was in the process of financing his fifth restaurant told me about this progression when he heard that I was involved with marketing.)

That's what happened to Nike. And it's happening with Starbucks (they're approaching that middle level). This is a precarious position for the brand because overexposure risks driving away the customer base that came of age hanging out at Starbucks. As a loyalist, I hope that they set their sights on maintaining their essence as a friendly, hip, coffee-intensive brand where you can get comfortable. It's going to happen to Altoids at some point, though they're trying hard to avoid it.

At midlevel, the brand has to tread carefully. You want to proliferate, you want to make more money, but by that same token you have to be cautious about how you do it.

The nimble brand strategist balances maintaining core equity and the needs of their most loyal customer segments with instituting changes necessary to keep ahead of shifts in the category and the priorities of the next generation of likely consumers. The brands that endure continually find ways to reinvigorate themselves. But the market is changing, too. Narrower and narrower customer segments based on values and attitudes as well as age, gender, income, and culture are looking for messages that speak to them on an emotional level. And with more channels of communication, they're looking in more diverse places.

The new millennium winners will address a fractionated consumer population. For some, it may mean developing different brand messages, positionings, and mediums to court each of those demographically and attitudinally diverse audiences. For others, it may result in targeting smaller consumer segments that promise a higher probability of an enduring relationship. Either way, brands risk extinction when they remain static while the world around them changes.

Paradigm Shifts

Every so often something happens to forever change the landscape in a category. The breath mint category was altered in the 1950s when chlorophyll entered the scene and the previously taboo problem of bad breath was out in the open and remedied with a piece of gum. It underwent a sea change when Tic Tac came along and the unique plastic container plus the minimint size took breath freshening further out in the open because we shared the "blast" with our friends. Then, there was Altoids, in a collectable tin, curiously strong, funky, sharable, and guaranteed to take care of coffee breath and anything else that we were jamming into our mouths those late nights in Seattle at the computer keyboard. Yet another paradigm shift gave birth to power mints, really tiny sugarless products.

In ice cream, the super creamy premiums exploded the category in the mid-1970s. Among the cognoscenti, Howard Johnson's was known to possess a top-notch, triple-rich ice cream that could have competed *mano a mano* with the heavy hitters. Instead of promoting its deluxe ice cream brand, HoJos went belly up keeping the secret to themselves. They could have been on a par with Häagen-Dazs. Instead they remained orange roofs.

The SPF factor revolutionized the suntan industry. Suddenly suntans were verboten as the category advanced from tanning to protection, from oils that promoted an even browning to lotions that blocked harmful rays. Gone was the Saint-Tropez tan, at least on this side of the ocean. It was smart to be white in July.

Snapple did it to soft drinks. Schwab did it to brokerage houses. Starbucks did it in coffee consumption. Once the competitive playing field is altered, it's easy to find your brand unprepared and ultimately wrong-footed.

In a broader sense, "natural" transformed entire supermarket shelves. When I started doing focus groups, there was no mandatory ingredient list that specified grams, percentages, and Minimum Daily Requirement unless the product was specially designed for people who wanted to watch their sugar or salt intake. (That section in the supermarket was cleverly labeled as dietetic.) But the wily consumer had figured out that the ingredients that were listed on the package were in descending order. The closer to the top of the list, the more there was of that ingredient in the product.

This is all very vivid in my memory because I was doing an enormous amount of work for Post Cereals in those days. Post has always struck me as a number two brand, and so it has a warm spot in my heart. Number twos are underdog brands. Avis was one of the first to make a campaign out of it by letting consumers know with buttons and slogans that "we're number two, we try harder." But the same kind of stigma exists in other categories. Chevrolet may be number two to Ford; Pepsi is number two to Coke.

At first, manufacturers turned their backs on the hippie mother throwbacks in each focus group who would extol the virtues of a nonprocessed diet. Clients sitting behind the one-way mirror in those days loved to comment that maybe a couple of women cared, but the sales of sugared cereal were soaring, and all of the fiber stuff was sitting on the shelf gathering dust.

Then Quaker surprised everyone who was pooh-poohing the growing consumer buzz about things natural and pure and launched a granola-like product called Quaker 100% Natural Cereal. Consumers were gobbling it up, and Post was left to play catch-up.

The Quaker product was so right in every regard, including the outrageous amount of natural sugars it contained to make it tasty, that I remember telling Post that my hypotheses and findings about how best to enter the market were embodied in the Quaker 100% Natural Cereal box: They pushed their brand name and didn't bother to come up with a sub brand. They could have called it "Harvest Morn" or "Sun Pure," for example, and put Quaker in mouse type. They stood forward and claimed the territory. They made natural even more prominent by putting it in the brand name (like Softsoap) and pumping it up with "100%." (In those days, consumers had yet to realize that 100 percent natural doesn't necessarily mean 100 percent beneficial. This was to happen in the next decade.)

They called it "cereal" because "granola" came with a lot of negative baggage, as I was learning in my own focus groups. It was associated with undesirable people who probably lived in communes. Those who had tried it from a health-food store found it to be too crunchy and it hurt their teeth. Sometimes it wasn't sweet enough. It didn't change character in milk like regular cereal. Quaker's response to this probable array of consumer comment, "Let's just call it cereal and get it out on the shelf."

Like a good marketer, Quaker realized that it had gold in its brand, and with consumers spending less time at home eating cereal out of a bowl, they wanted to make it more portable. Hence, the birth of Quaker 100% Granola Bars.

But, this product wasn't quite the messiah the marketers had anticipated. It looked like a candy bar and it was packaged like a candy bar, but it tasted like a cereal and it was far too crunchy. Sure it was natural, but if I want a candy bar, do I really want it to be natural? Quaker went back to their benches and made it more like candy. They came out with peanut butter varieties, added chocolate to everything, I think there was even a marshmallow flavor. This infuriated consumers even more. Now in groups, I heard that Quaker 100% Natural Cereal had let the consumers down. They had stood out in the forefront of the natural phenomenon and established a certain amount of consumer trust, then lost it by calling candy bars "natural."

Now there's another power play in the bar section. Power Bars have given birth to a whole array of bars that differentiate themselves from candy bars because they are, by their nature, beneficial. They are being devoured based on the benefits they offer: energy, high protein, fiber, low carbohydrates. Taste would almost seem secondary.

In the 1980s, Nabisco saw the earth move under its feet with its Healthy Choice brand. The emerging consumer enemy in the Reagan years was fat. We wanted to be slim and slender and were convinced that anything that had fat was to be avoided. And the consumer was buying into it all. Nabisco hit pay dirt. It transformed the snack world by introducing Healthy Choice and even nailed the fat-free color as green.

Healthy Choice was being written about in every marketing industry magazine as the brand winner and collected numerous awards. Then, the consumer started reading labels seriously and learned that even though fat-free might have less fat, it could have more calories and, gasp, yes, even more sugar in some cases. I started hearing the word-of-mouth hum in focus groups as one consumer told another that this brand was a fraud and that they felt duped.

Healthy Choice is still around. Over the years, the brands expanded from cookies to frozen entrées. I hear about it in frozen entrée work that I occasionally do for Stouffer's. The main associations consumers now make with it: "That's the one in the green box, right? It's expensive and the portions are small. You know, even though something is fat-free, it still has a lot of calories. Have you read the ingredients label?"

My Generation

Yes, you want consumers to be loyal. No, you don't want to grow old and tired because of them. How will Loving Care prevent its image from going graying? How can Maxwell House keep stride with the Starbucks generation that sips latte on the run? I haven't done any Maxwell House work in a while, but their "good to the last drop" revamp seems on target. Whoever is doing their groups is encouraging the brand to listen and take advantage of its memorable slogan while it's still memorable and means quality. I think they rescued it just before it might have sunk into oblivion along with Speedy Alka Seltzer and the Jolly Green Giant.

If any brand was poised to go from generation to generation, surely Levi's, nearly synonymous with jeans for over 125 years, could have done it. For whatever reasons, they didn't respond wisely to recent shifts in that mercurial entity, teen taste. The Gap triumvirate of Gap, Banana Republic, and Old Navy stole the hip trouser business from this venerable brand by providing different cultures, retail concepts, and price points, leaving stale old Levi's blue as blue can be.

Now, the Gap trio sets the pants leg length and flare, the waist/hip fit, and seems to have something for everyone without losing their identity. But in some city, around some table, a group of young people more than likely is examining new concepts for some other type of leg garment, or distribution opportunity, or attitude . . . maybe even from Levi's. There is no brand immunity; a lesson I relearn repeatedly.

Another case in point: Coppertone. For me, nothing spells summer quite like the smell of Coppertone. It's the quintessential brand. The name instantly evokes warmth and beach and a tanned, pigtailed cherub with a puppy pulling at her bathing suit to reveal a white bottom. Not so for consumers in their 20s. Studying suntan products, I found that Coppertone registered as just another face in the SPF crowd. Rival Bain de Soleil did not have a strong image, but at least consumers thought it sounded sophisticated and European. Coppertone was lifeless, inert; even I was surprised to see how far the brand of my youth had fallen.

In the same vein, I did a project in which Audrey Hepburn represented the essence of style for a brand's proposed print campaign. Half of the groups in their 20s and 30s weren't sure who she was. "What's her name? I know I've seen her." Then someone older would fill in, Audrey Hepburn. "Oh yeah, I always get them confused, Audrey Hepburn, Katharine Hepburn." If they don't know who she is, how can she represent style?

One generation's symbols and badges rarely translate to another generation. We reserve a special place for the reference points of our youth, which frequently makes me question whether baby boomers assigned to market brands to younger generations should bow out of the act. Likewise, advertising executives in their 20s and 30s should step aside from marketing to seniors. How many times can a senior consumer be expected to relate to a picture of a mature man and a mature women, standing by their bicycles on a clear autumn day about to decide on supplementary health insurance? Or, how many 20-year-olds are really going to want to read about a brand because a youthful person is surfing through a print ad on a skateboard?

Marketers often totally underestimate college students. Reaching college-age consumers requires acknowledging who they are and understanding that they're walking a line where they're half children, half adults. They're likely to lose their student ID once a week; yet by the same token, they view themselves as responsible, mature citizens living on their own with serious responsibilities.

College kids study and analyze anything that you put forth and one thing they know is how to work the system. They've been marketed to and exposed to so much that they're a cynical lot. If you're going to offer them any promotion that has any kind of loophole, or it has any way at all of being misused, they'll figure it out. If you're going to give them free air travel for using a credit card, they'll probably give their credit card to all their friends to use, have their friends give them cash, pay the bill, rack up the miles, and fly home free. They like beating the system.

What college students do respond to is grassroots marketing. Finding out about a brand from other college students in some underground way, which is what happened with microbreweries, feeds their sense of superiority. Striking a hip, irreverent tonality without condescension—think Budweiser campaigns—at least draws their attention. To hang out with this cliquish crowd, a brand also needs the right associations. Having a Visa card sticking out of the back pocket of the coolest brand of cargo pants won't register, but sponsoring a Shaggy concert tour might.

Even with brands looking to hit a broad target, attitudinal differences increasingly come into play when considering how to woo the consumer with lasting power. I've done lots of work with laundry products and the different approaches to this ordinary chore are telling. At one end of the spectrum, you have the folks who take their dirty clothes, jam them into the machine, throw in some detergent, turn it on, remember several hours later to transfer the stuff to the dryer and then to take it out a couple of days later. Or the families with lots of kids, who do 20 loads a week and it's in, out, done, gone.

At the opposite end are women extraordinarily involved in their laundry. They take each item, look at it beforehand, and worry over every stain. They separate colors and fabrics very deliberately, fill the machine a certain way—water, then detergent, then clothes—do smaller loads, use gentle cycle versus regular, add specific additives at precise times. They make lots of decisions throughout the whole process. And when they take the clothes out exactly 32 minutes after they put it in, they examine the clothes very carefully and if the stain isn't gone, repeat the process again, thinking "Thank God I haven't put them in the dryer yet, because it will really set if I get it in the dryer." They never blame the product; they blame themselves.

These antithetical attitudes surfaced again when I was investigating concepts for one of those laundry stain removers that involved different degrees of convenience from *here's the stick of stuff, find the spot, work on it,* through *throw this tablet in every wash and it will automatically and magically get rid of any stains because it has special sensors to locate stains and remove them.* We divided the groups by degree of laundry obsession. The groups that used one product of course loved being able to throw something into the machine and say, "Okay, if it works, it works; I don't give a damn." The women who had complex laundry rituals were aghast at the idea of just tossing a tablet in: "If I'm not involved, the spot will never come out. Why should I trust the product? I have to get in there."

We found the real motivating factor was control. If they weren't an active part of the process, nothing would work. If you entered a person's home who fell under the control category, you would probably find multiple additives. These are the brand loyalists. Whereas in the non-control group you'd find a box of detergent, and maybe bleach for whites. The brand would be whatever they had a coupon for that month. (By the by, if they both had been in the same group, we might have left with a distorted perspective.)

These variations in attitude should affect which product the manufacturer decides to develop and to whom and how to target its marketing. How many women use pretreats? Say it's 30 percent of the population. That's a big percentage, and if company executives are smart, for the time being, they'll forget about the 70 percent that don't because it's too hard to change behavior. Go after the women who use pretreats and would be the most interested in this concept. And when that product is developed, talk to them about control: *You know only you can get that stain out and this is an aid that will help you accomplish that.* Win her over and you have a lifetime fan for this product and a potential one for your next.

Dollars and Census

The 2000 census reconfirmed the multicultural nature of the U.S. marketplace. This is not new news, yet advertisers and marketers have been absurdly slow in reacting. The rapid growth of minority populations should serve as a warning shot that unless you find a better way to talk to racially and ethnically diverse populations, you will be talking to yourself.

I'm often embarrassed by the whiteness of our advertising. Rarely do I get any commercials to test in storyboard form that have any faces of color or anything ethnic. If there is, it's self-consciously done, seemingly added at the last moment because someone realized that they better include an Asian, Hispanic, African American. The eyes are a little too slanted, the colors unrealistic shades, or just sepia tones. It's very embarrassing to show these executions in a group where there are people of color. When I ask them to talk to me about this ad, people of color say—and it's hard for them to be frank with me because I'm white—"I'll tell you Bonnie, I'm a black woman and I don't understand why those two pair of bare feet sticking out from under that blanket in that ad are white. That's not me." In consumerspeak, "That's not me," means "You are irrelevant." If you are irrelevant to the consumer, you are invisible.

Only in the past few years have many large corporations instituted diversity departments, as much to exploit untapped and possibly lucrative markets as to be upstanding citizens. With some noticeable exceptions like fast food, beer, and snacks, and cleaning products, companies have generally confined efforts to reflect diversity in their marketing and advertising to brands specifically aimed at minority populations or in minority media.

Part of the reason for the lack of color in mainstream media is that ad agencies are still predominantly white. The growth in specialty agencies and divisions has begun to address questions of how to reach these populations with messages that are linguistically and culturally relevant. Meanwhile, the elephant in the room remains the fear of turning off white audiences.

In groups, the message from minorities is *if you want me, show me you know me.* Research indicates that minorities, whether Chinese, African Americans, Indians, or Filipinos, are more prone to buy brands that feature a person like themselves in an ad. As a bonus, minority groups tend to be extremely brand conscious and loyal.

Minority audiences are inured to seeing advertising that excludes them. Tic Tacs used to have Kelly Harmon, white, blond, cheerleader type, as a spokesperson. Currently, they have a carbon copy doing the job. I was doing individual depth interviews on this new advertising and some of the sample were African Americans, solid breath-mint users. I have to say, "How do you feel about this spokeswoman? Talk to me a little about her." There's a pause. I can tell by one woman's body language that what she wants to say is, "That white girl looks like that other white girl."

What does she actually say? A chatty black woman with big hoop earrings and beautiful long dreads offers up the typical response: "She seems personable, nice, perky. She's okay." My interpretation of the comments: "This is not an ad for African Americans but there's nothing wrong with this girl. She's not arrogant or snooty. I don't have anything against her." For the advertiser, it means she can span the racial or ethnic divide. This merely confirms that minimum level of acceptability among the black Tic Tac consuming market.

Nice 'n Easy hair coloring was looking for new fodder for another advertising campaign for the brand. We were set to do groups in Washington, D.C., to gain some insights and find a new way of talking about the product. The company knew that they had a large black franchise and decided to include this segment in the research to see if they could tap any new learning for the advertising.

As it turned out, the sessions were on the eve of the Rodney King verdict and here I was a white woman about to talk to black women about coloring their hair, a sensitive subject to begin with. I decided to bite the bullet and just asked the women if they had been following the news and how they felt about the whole Rodney King situation. It was worth spending 15 minutes to just air it out, exchange opinions, and get everybody talking. Then I was able to shut it down and say, "I'd like to talk to you all night, but let's get into the reason we're actually here." It worked and was one of the best groups I ever did. We discussed how fragile and weak black hair actually is and how black hair products, pastes, gels, straighteners, and color are hard to locate and ghettoize in drugstore aisles. I doubt that any of this affected the final Clairol Nice 'n Easy strategy, but I learned a lot about dealing with sensitive situations by pressing on.

I guess that it's a question of money and wanting to reach the broadest audience without alienating anyone. Minority groups are so accustomed to seeing white that to a large extent they can put themselves into that position. Whites will not do the reverse. They won't put themselves into the black audience. If a white woman is looking for hair coloring and sees a commerical with two black women talking about how great their hair looks, she ignores what they say. It's not relevant to the white audience. This is no big surprise. Imagine how relevant that same situation could be with a diverse population. But to establish the points of relevance, you have to listen to the differences. The differences may represent opportunity.

Selection of media has become the preferred way to reach minority markets. If you pick up a copy of *Essence* or *Jet* you will see the same brands as advertised in *Cosmopolitan*, but adapted to fit the needs of a different readership. American Express is a genius at segmenting their advertising dollar, but they have sufficient money to spread around. So does McDonald's. They're hitting all fronts by virtue of smart media selection.

The same remarks could be addressed for the gay and lesbian community. Only recently has corporate America realized that gays and lesbians with higher incomes and fewer kids are a hot marketing niche. With the stamp of approval from shows like *Ellen* and *Will & Grace*, businesses have felt freer to zero in on this potential gold mine, though they still mainly confine their efforts to gay-oriented media.

But without any effort to cement relationships with minority groups, a company leaves its brand vulnerable to attack by a brand willing to make preference and color-blind moves. What might have been a secure position can easily turn into a revolving door. Product purchase is only one step in establishing a firm connection between consumer and brand. In a highly multicultural world, it may be the weakest link.

Global Village

When you're looking through the results of a focus group on shampoos conducted by Colgate in Thailand, it suddenly hits how small the world has become. Global corporations jump across borders with ease; however, that doesn't guarantee that the way you position and market your brand in Rome, Italy, will work as effectively in Rome, New York.

The focus group dynamic itself is different from country to country and from culture to culture. More global research means that we have to rely on our partners in other countries to alert us to any cultural differences that may affect group outcome. We can't just take one questionnaire, literally translate it into five languages, and assume that we will get the same panelists in all countries.

Americans tend to be garrulous and outspoken. We like to have our opinions heard and we like to use colorful language to express ourselves. We are, after all, a country where the rugged individualist can succeed against all odds. In France, it's not un-common to have three-hour groups because at least an hour is taken up in niceties and dining. In Italy, the passion of opinions can draw out the sessions. Americans get right to the point.

Cultural differences crop up in strange places. Rémy Martin was set to introduce a new brand of cognac in the United States that had been popular in Japan. In Asia, it was called Club and was in the high-end price range. Prior to launching it in the United States, Rémy executives thought an examination of New Yorkers' reaction to the new spirit would be prudent. We did depth interviews to see if Club had legs among the affluent in New York as it did in Tokyo.

Many Japanese companies like American, Anglo-Saxon sounding words, regardless of meaning. For the Japanese clientele, the word Club denotes elitism, an exclusive place to visit. But when it comes to wines and cognac, Americans want to hear French. In beverage terms, club is club soda. Club is more base-ball and beer than cut crystal snifters after dinner. The cognac fans we talked to ranked Club at the bottom of any names that might stand for quality. The U.S. preference leaned toward Rémy

Martin, Hennessey, or niche specialty brands. In the end, I don't know if they ever came out with the product under another name, but what I do know is that without this research, there would probably be something on the shelf labeled Club Cognac that only a Japanese consumer visiting the United States would buy.

The Italian candy maker Ferrero makes an absolutely delicious product called Rocher. You see a lot of it during the holidays. It's round, gold foil-wrapped chocolate with a hazelnut filling. Our job was to gauge how an American audience responded to a commercial produced for an Italian audience. If it worked, there would be no need to develop new advertising, and valuable monies could be allocated into other areas.

The commercial features a chichi party in which a butler comes out carrying a tray of Rocher stacked in a pyramid to offer the guests. The Italians in this case perceive that the great charm and allure of Rocher attracts the considerate host or hostess, who aspires to serve this pyramid of fine chocolates. It works well in Italy and the rest of Europe.

When I showed the commercial to American focus groups, the immediate response was: "Who gives a party like that? I don't entertain like that." Americans usually don't put candy out for parties unless it's for a big holiday, like Christmas or Easter and then because they've received the candy as a gift. They think putting candy out is formal and very Martha Stewart.

I can ignore some of that as a moderator because we all aspire to more luxurious lifestyles. But when I said, "Just tell me what's in your mind about that commercial," what a woman in one group said (and this reaction was repeated in group after group), "Did you see that look on the woman's face when she ate it? The guest really seems to enjoy it. Must be really good candy." By sheer accident, the producer of the commercial had a guest take one of the candies, eat a bite, and swoon. It was incidental because the Italians produced the commercial from the host's point of view. *If I want to give a great party, I should serve Rocher candy.*

In the United States, the perspective was that of the guest. *She enjoyed eating that candy so much, I'll bet it's delicious and I will buy it for me as an indulgence.* Every focus group zeroed in on this one elegant woman with upswept hair who daintily takes a bite of the chocolate. Americans said things like "I'd throw the whole thing in my mouth, partly because I don't want anyone to know I'm eating it, it's a kind of guilty pleasure." They also admitted that they would "take three or four and put them in my purse."

While we went into the project certain that the commercial wouldn't work with an American audience, it actually performs quite well, if not for the expected reasons, and has served the brand admirably for several holiday seasons. The Italian contingent is happy to know that they produced a globally winning commercial; the client who listened, understands why, and when it's time to really strategize an American story for Rocher, we'll have the right perspective to work with.

Brand Resurrection

All is not lost for those seemingly obsolete brands. The good news for moribund brands is that the consumer memory is short and, as hot pants, *Charlie's Angels,* and game shows prove, everything old can be new again. Some brands can ride back in on a wave of nostalgia or take advantage of years of absence to reposition themselves. We think consumers will remember why they disappeared, but more times than not, they don't. If you have a comatose brand, don't be so anxious to pull the plug. In 10 years, or even 5, the whole world may change again. My advice is to go back, dust the cobwebs off neglected brands, and test for signs of life.

"There are no tired brands; there are only tired brand managers," the president and chief executive of Unilever declared when he announced a campaign for an old product in a new guise—laundry tablets, missing in action since the late 1970s—under the Wisk umbrella. He's right.

Mr. Bubble rose phoenix-like when the Restoration Hardware folks, always on the lookout to resurrect products from baby boomers' youth, added the bubble bath to its nostalgia wares. Poor Mr. Bubble suffered through one of those paradigm shifts when Disney came out and said to the manufacturers that made this stuff that's comparable to dish detergent (in fact, parents often fill the empties with dishwashing liquid), you can license our characters. Then it became the Winnie the Pooh line for the bath. And when *Beauty and the Beast* was big, every little girl had to have a Belle bubble bath. *Sesame Street* licensed their characters so all the really little kids, who didn't want Belle, wanted the Cookie Monster. Nobody wanted Mr. Bubble until somebody realized he had kitsch value, especially in the box.

Before the kitsch appeal, I had done a study to see how far our client could push the Mr. Bubble personality. Bottles were designed that had him in scuba gear, in dude surfing shorts with sunglasses, and other outlandish configurations. What we heard from Moms was that they liked the simplicity and uninflated price of the basic Mr. Bubble bottle and character. For really tiny tots, Mr. Bubble was as intriguing as the Cookie Monster.

At this second in time, stainless-steel streamlined versions of the old scooters seem ready to reach their apex, soon to be tossed in the back of the closet with our old Rollerblades. Like hula hoops, yo-yos, and many other fads, they will ride again. Pop Rocks come to mind. As I understand it, this is actually no more than a gelatin-based powder product that's got some kind of encapsulated carbonation to produce a fizzing, popping sensation in your mouth.

I was drawn like much of the Woodstock generation, to anything that promised a mood or physical change. When I grew up and became a moderator, the product reappeared from General Foods (now absorbed by Kraft Foods) and was appealing to a new generation. General Foods realized this was not a long-term business like Jell-O, but they could make good use of a technology they owned with a new generation of children who didn't know that their parents had also craved this back-of-mouth popping. The brand people decided to go out full force with grand flavor arrays, sell millions, and then let the business die its due death when kids tired of it.

My advice to whoever owns this product now is, guess what? There's a new generation on the horizon, and it may be time to resurrect this fad one more time. If it were my brand, I might go the Mr. Bubble route and distribute a few hundred cases through Restoration Hardware.

Other brands might take a page from Herbal Essence, the funky shampoo from the 1970s. It was intensely fragrant to appeal to the earth goddess in us. By the mid-1980s, our passion had waned for heavy-duty liquid detergent shampoo with that flower-power kick. Herbal Essence looked like it was headed for early retirement.

But Clairol decided to give the shampoo an image makeover. They updated the packaging, downplayed the intense fragrance and a sexy independent woman took over for earth mother. In the commercials, our 1990s user was a woman—perhaps on a business trip—washing her hair in an airplane bathroom. Her *When Harry Met Sally* oohs and aahs of orgasmic delight as she lathered up aroused the rapt attention of the other passengers. Quite a shocking departure for Clairol, owned by the stodgy drug company Bristol-Myers.

I got a chance to see how the new plan was working when Clairol called me in to test if they should extend the Herbal Essence line into a body wash. I thought this was the logical next step, but first I wanted to hear people's reaction to the commercial. Because I was familiar with the old Herbal Essence, I expected everybody, in all of the groups I did with women from 18 to 54, to say: "Oh yeah, that old green stuff that they put in a different bottle and changed the color and fragrance. Do you really think because you gave Herbal Essence a new cachet, I won't remember that awful smelly stuff?" They didn't. They loved the commercials. They loved the fragrances. They loved the packaging. The whole allure of the brand had shifted to being a fresh and natural experiential delight. I strongly recommended that they come out with the body wash. It was a dynamite extension of the new Herbal Essence brand. It's on the market now, this time with the erotic fantasy taking place in an elevator and an extra push by sexpert Dr. Ruth. Fueled by a gutsy campaign, Clairol successfully repositioned Herbal Essence shampoo. In fact, the brand has come up with a hair color. Good going Clairol.

The master of bringing brands back from the dead is a guy named Jeffrey Himmel, who breathed life into such brands as Ovaltine, Doan's Pills, and Gold Bond. His philosophy is simple and direct. When Himmel took over Ovaltine in 1992, the first ads went something like: "When was the last time you tried Ovaltine? Ovaltine helps me get going every morning, it's good nutrition. Just two glasses of Ovaltine contains more than 10 essential vitamins and minerals. There's nothing quite like Ovaltine. It tastes great and it's really good for you." It couldn't be more basic.

Over the years, they have not evolved much either. In one of their latest campaigns, a man comes into a house and says:

"Hey, let's have Nestlé's Quik."

His son replies: "Dad, Quik's out."

Then the daughter chimes in: "We switched to rich chocolate Ovaltine."

To which, Dad asks: "Why?"

Wise Mom sets the record straight: "Ovaltine's better for you. It has vitamins and minerals, Quik doesn't."

The little girl adds (for what's known as taste reinforcement): "And it tastes great."

Dad gives his seal of approval: "Mmm, it is great."

And finally in unison, the family says: "More Ovaltine please."

What's interesting about this simple advertising is that Himmel believes that what you mainly have to do is keep saying your brand name and keep emphasizing why people should get it. Ovaltine sales are picking up. All those brands trying to be so abstract are spending millions of dollars for no action. Nothing's happening. The consumer is not buying it.

Himmel floods the network. The advertising is straight out of the 1950s. There's no memorable gimmick, no fancy lines, just the repetition of the brand and its essential core point of difference hammered home again and again. It's whatever happened to . . . and then you see hundreds of ads. They're in all of the magazines; you're being swamped with coupons. Every time you turn on the radio, somebody is mentioning it. The television commercials are sort of funky, but you remember the brand.

In the beginning, he advertises it by saying, "You haven't thought about it for a while, have you, but it's really great, it'll give you energy." And that evolves in several years to, "We're better than the competition, because we're better for you and we taste good, too." Himmel takes the backbone of what a brand stands for and sticks to it. I'm not saying that every advertiser should do it, but it's important today for manufacturers to realize that simplicity has its place.

Not all faded brands can be brought back to life, nor should they be. The smarter road to travel: Avoid possible extinction in the first place by watching for the early warning signs of change. Brands that remain static while the world around them changes will find themselves facing Oldsmobile's fate. Using focus groups is one way to explore aspects of shifts in attitude, the segmenting of society, or upheavals in the marketplace and their implications for a brand. Companies must keep up with—and capitalize on— new developments and changing mind-sets and patterns in consumer behavior.

LISTENING POINTS

- ◎ Even powerful brands cannot rest on their laurels.
- ◎ Listen with your competitor's ears and interests as well as your own.
- ◎ A brand is most vulnerable when it is successful.
- ◎ Brands need reinvigoration from time to time. Staleness is the kiss of death.
- ◎ When the paradigm shifts, so should you.
- ◎ Usually, the loud voices of a few consumers at the fringe become a reality within a generation. Be prepared. Watch them grow and try to meet them halfway.
- ◎ The mass market is not white and will never be white again.
- ◎ Market to your target consumers in a language and with symbols and values that are meaningful to them.
- ◎ Even in a small world, the differences matter.
- ◎ Virtually any brand can be resurrected.

13

HAVE YOU HEARD

Trends for the New Millennium

As a rule, predictions are best left to the likes of Nostradamus. Forecasting doesn't seem to be any more successful with quarterly sales figures than with weather reports. No sooner do you report on a trend than it plateaus or wanes. What looks like a movement may turn out to be nothing more than a fad, meaningless unless you were smart enough to start it in the first place. While the Internet as a source of instant and comprehensive information is here to stay, the "e"-ing of everything turned out to be merely a fad, aimlessly surfing is no more entertaining than thumbing through a phone book.

With that caveat, I look ahead in this chapter and discuss a few ideas and trends that are gaining momentum, based on the subterranean murmurings I hear in talking and listening to a wide swath of the consuming public.

Convenience

The definition of convenience will undergo a radical transformation. It will no longer mean that it's just easy to do, to prepare, or to use in taking care of home and family. Convenience will involve providing products and services that consumers can use and do whenever they choose and wherever they are.

Whenever we leave home, we take our lives along. Female panelists enter my focus groups across the country laden with enormous bags. Purses have given way to large sacks that contain all the necessary equipment for daily survival.

In urban areas among consumers in their 20s and 30s, this survival kit is likely to include colorful and small electronic devices: cell phone, beeper, PDAs, MP3 players, and the attendant tangle of earpieces and wires. The problem compounds for parents contending with their own must-haves and those of their children.

In focus groups I did in the Chicago suburbs in mid-2001, one of the proposed new commercials focused on a woman who was loading up her purse. The commercial showed her packing in a phone, her Palm Pilot, and her beeper. Women with children pointed out that any form of electronic equipment except their cell phone was irrelevant in their lives. But be sure to show a young mother packing up hand wipes, tissues, small toys, crayons, and snacks to dole out to attention-challenged children.

While magazine articles and television segments may be predicting a future where we all will need a utility belt to carry our electronic devices, the electronic age as a portable phenomenon is still the bailiwick of frequent business travelers, the technocrats, and the latest breed of yuppies who have emerged from the cocoons of Generation X. Since most of the trend analysis comes from major urban areas, this electronic phenomenon may be overstated. In the center of the country or in many suburbs, the trends are quite different. The electronic soothsaying that depicts homes and offices equipped with universal recharge stations may be in the distant future. In the more immediate future, manufacturers in all categories, including packaged goods, should think small. We want things that are smaller, lighter to fit in purses, backpacks, briefcases, pockets, from minisize Altoids to bitesize snacks.

Any packaging work I do where the wrapping is extraneous meets with significant consumer distaste. Streamlined and efficient packaging that's also friendly to use rates high marks. This means trigger sprays that don't tire the hands and drink boxes that not only come with their own straw but can also be easily poured.

Food manufacturers should reexamine the portions that they make available to consumers. Whole families may sit down to a meal at the same time when vigilant parents insist on mealtime as a time to communicate with their youngsters. The rest of us are having take-out, food on the run. If you want to make our lives even easier, provide all the utensils we need to eat it, and then allow us to feel good about disposing of it because it doesn't have a lot of excess packaging.

More and more consumers leave home in the morning, grab everything needed for the day, and may not return until it's dark. Plus, we spend an inordinate amount of time in our home on wheels. Automobile manufacturers have been wise enough to realize that we drink from cups of many sizes but still haven't found a place for a woman's purse or anyone's knapsack. Who doesn't eat in the car these days? Add children to the equation and the car is transformed into a mobile fast-food outlet. Our automobiles should not be overlooked as the new frontier for products like hard surface cleaners, upholstery cleaners, carpet cleaners, dust repellants, fabric refreshers, bug repellants, and antibacterial sprays.

In terms of service, we already have 24-hour hot lines. What we'd prefer are interactions with real people, or at least improved loop lines that actually get some action before the company attempts to sell us something, feed us automated database information, or have us input account numbers repeatedly. I talked to a friend recently hired to devise perpetual loop phone lines, menus purposefully designed to result in nothing. The circuits never got callers to an actual person, but just swung them around and around.

This wouldn't seem as annoying if we thought it was just a personnel shortage. The endless telemarketing solicitation calls we all receive tell us where corporations have chosen to staff up. On many occasions, the only way I have gotten action is to press the menu number that indicates I can find out more about products and services offered by this company. I know that a sales rep is waiting there, thinking he will take my order, and I can plead with an actual human for help.

A waitress who collected huge tips once told me her secret: On the busiest of nights, all she had to do was give the customers rolls and water and tell them that she'd be right back. It's a token kindness of future intention that the impatient diner can relate to. The reward will go to those companies who separate themselves from the thousands of others that think that all they need is an 800-number, a menu of options, the reminder that "this call may be monitored," and cloying background music interspersed with the same smooth-toned voice that attempts to soothe our growing rage by telling us that our call is, indeed, important.

Based on the disgust and frustration I hear from the U.S. consumer toward the dreaded 800-number, companies better look to their problem-solving skills. Why not take all of the telemarketers and turn them into "teleconveyors" who would act as personal intermediaries between the customers and whoever holds the answers.

Here's what consumers tell me they're after: I don't care if I can't speak to someone in charge, but I do want to get some action from someone who will be compassionate enough and smart enough to really understand my problem and help solve it. When I call back, I want to be able to speak to that same personal representative who helped me the first time. I don't want to have to repeat my tale of woe to the next guy who happens to pick up. I want 24-hour contact and a person on the 2 A.M. shift as smart as the one on the more popular 2 P.M. shift.

If corporations can train their people to sell anything to anyone, why not use this same training philosophy to instill compassion and consideration in their workforce? As much as we are becoming accustomed to computer-generated advice and answers, we also crave the human touch, someone to act between human and machine. Deliver here and you've won the consumer's heart.

American Express already excels in this area. Even Amex bashers admit that when and if they ever lost a card, Amex was there with a compassionate voice to work them through the rigors of getting a new card wherever they were.

Comforting Thoughts

A commercial for an upscale hotel chain promises that if you are a frequent guest, they will make sure that your favorite toothpaste, flowers, and magazines are in your room and your preferred pillow style and linen colors are on the bed before you check in. Road warriors are stressed out because travel eliminates routine. Business travelers favor the same brand of hotel because they know how the room key activates the door, they recognize the remote, the shampoo has a familiar fragrance, and the decor is the same from city to city. All of this routine provides the traveler with comfort. And comfort and simplicity are what everyone is seeking in this millennium. As the most sophisticated and discerning group of consumers, business travelers are the first to fall into line for this positioning of comfort, simplicity, and the promise to make their time away seem more like home.

In the bigger picture, the very meaning of "home" is changing. We have home pages and bookmark favorite places to replicate the comfort of coming home. Home represents desired routine. Whenever I do research with married women with young children, I'm amazed how many seem to dislike summer because it interferes with their routines. As chaotic as any home is when children are around, during the school year, there's a schedule of events. Children struggle out of bed, get dressed, lunches are packed, pets are fed, all within roughly the same time frame from day to day. Bring on the warmer weather when school's out, and the day is up for grabs.

A psychologist who is a friend of mine has a theory that we all exhibit some form of obsessive-compulsive behavior disorder. Some of us panic if our dresser drawers aren't perfectly well ordered; others of us freak out if our desk has been rearranged. One of my clients insists that all of his staff staple documents on the right side. A Fortune 100 CEO once admitted that he saved every paper clip he removed and would paw through his trash if one inadvertently slipped through his fingers.

As a researcher, I'm always wondering why. And my conclusion about the obsessive consumer is that he or she needs routine in his life. We don't realize how important daily sameness is until it's removed. When suddenly we don't have time to grind the beans for our coffee, get the car washed on Tuesdays, or read our *New York Times* during lunch, these rituals become all-important.

We may like to be told when and how to do things more so than the modern marketer may think. Choice used to be the big word. But to the same extent that proliferation is driving us crazy, we cherish a certain degree of sameness.

Variety is great, but please give us some advice about what to choose and be more precise about the real differences in our options. AOL continues to stay ahead of the crowd because it's ubiquitous and simple; we can find it anywhere, anytime, and our home page will look roughly the same each time we log on.

Gateway's current ad campaign is positioned around the concept that you have a friend at the company who really knows your name and order and will follow through for you, from checking for components to shipping out the custom model. If you're a repeat visitor at the Ritz Carlton in Washington, D.C., the hotel monograms your pillowcases and sends them home with you as a gift.

We're entering a new age of "customerization," where what you know about me as a consumer is converted into highly personal benefits. Computers give us the ability to gather and store incredible amounts of information about our likes and dislikes, our tendencies and attitudes, and our work habits and leisure activities. Like the Cheers bar, where everybody knows your name and your steady drink, megastores can draw on our profile to pamper us with personalized service and selections.

By that same token, it's okay to know who we are, but don't assume that you know all about us. If my surname happens to be Irish, don't assume that I'll want to be wished Happy St. Patrick's Day if I place an order on March 17th. Assumptions like this strike the consumer as intrusive. Ask permission before you put us on your list. The insurance and financial industries have initiated stricter privacy policies, and my advice to all marketers is follow their lead. Use your databases sensibly, judiciously, and sensitively.

Like too much of anything, customization can quickly lose its cachet of specialness. When every bellhop in every Marriott is welcoming me by name, asking me about my flight from O'Hare, and setting up two cans of caffeine-free diet Coke, I wonder what else they may know about me that I don't want them to know. Customization gives rise to concerns of privacy, greater isolationism, and reluctance to be forthcoming. Wisely used, it's a genuine touch of service; misused, it's Big Brother.

Partnership Agreements

Skilled marketers will no longer see the consumer simply as a human being who consumes, a one-way implication. Instead, he or she will be reconsidered as a collaborator, a two-way proposition: a person who is in on the action and who has as much of a vested interest in representing the brand as in using the brand. *The New York Times* comes closest to this in my experience; the involvement of its loyalists is so great that they see themselves as an essential part of the paper: "*The New York Times* is me; I am *The New York Times.*"

This new partnership arises because American consumers have become so savvy that they have almost an insider perspective on marketing. They can second-guess corporate and brand intentions before the top brass approves the strategy. With the eye of a cynic, they instantly spot loopholes and suspect problems. Twenty years ago, we would excuse these panelists from our focus group discussions because they seemed to know more than we wanted them to know. We assumed that they were professional panelists, or that their marketing smarts indicated they were involved with or had a good friend in the business. Today, I encourage clients to listen harder to these consumers and respect their comments.

Nowadays, we all know everything. If you want to be an expert, you better darn well prove it to us, because we will grill you to see if you really know as much as you claim. The glut of insider, behind-the-scenes media and information is making us all aware of everything in nanoseconds. It's difficult to shut up the savvy panelist in a focus group who is telling you how your client should market her new facial toner when the panelist's idea is better than your client's.

I was recently showing a mixed group of non-*Times* readers some *New York Times* advertising that featured Maya Angelou's voice-over. The few who recognized her voice assumed that the advertising was directed toward African Americans because the newspaper probably felt that its image was too white and was now going after a more diverse group. True or not, 10 years ago this same group of panelists would not have reached this conclusion. Instead, they might have responded to what Maya Angelou was saying rather than analyzing why she had been hired and scripted to say it.

The Graying Baby Boomer

As this generation slowly and steadily grows older, it will not be aging gracefully—no going gentle into that good night. This generation born in the decade after World War II will not put up with the likes of not seeing, not hearing, or losing its memory. Any drug or device that can forestall the process, improve it, or best yet, eliminate it, has got to be a winner. Consider all of the other aging things that we have long associated with the elderly and then think about how you can market remedies that suit the body-conscious, status-conscious, age-conscious baby boomer. A short list of ailments needing products in the next five years might include earwax, thinning hair, constipation, leg cramps, droopy jowls, toenail fungus.

What all of these represent to the boomers are inconveniences that get in the way. Don't discount the phenomenon that baby boomers were the first to freely talk about their innermost everything in consciousness-raising groups of the 1970s. If there is a product that does what it claims, or promises to help, chances are that one baby boomer will quickly tell another. As a member of that generation, I know how openly we discuss our menopause and impotence, our sagging breasts, and our hard stools. We'll admit to prostate problems and let you know that we're going through a bout of depression since we were laid off, and we're having trouble finding a job so we're thinking about getting rid of the gray to look like the young fellows who are being hired instead. Indeed, hairdressers in my groups tell me that men are showing up for hair-coloring advice by the hordes, which leads me to believe barbershops should hire color consultants.

Aging is an inconvenience, and we're not prepared to deal with its concomitant problems in the same way we saw our parents dealing with them. Take farsightedness. Not being able to see close up interferes more with my ability to know whether I'm pushing play or rewind on my VCR, and is less of a nuisance with reading. If I'm likely to be reading, I probably have planned to have my glasses nearby. It's all the unplanned events when we want to see that are interferences.

In advertising, acknowledge the inconvenience of aging rather than the typical consequences and problems of getting old. Spend time on the results and benefits rather than on problem elaboration.

Since boomers have style, you can be sure we'll be seeing more lorgnettes and magnifiers worn as ornaments. Folding glasses so slender that they look like nothing more than a good fountain pen are popping up all over. For our vanity and instant perfect vision, a laser operation seems a simple enough procedure. Sell it with a five-year renewal procedure and you'll have a loyalist.

We can't assume that people in their 60s at the beginning of the twenty-first century are going to be the same as people in their 60s in the twentieth century, anymore than we can assume that teenagers today have the same values and problems as previous generations of teenagers. There's certainly a chronological reality to aging, but there's also a perceptual reality, and this is the learning to keep in mind when marketing to different age groups.

Listen to how consumers talk about their lives and how they visualize themselves. In most cases, this sense of self is very different from what others may observe. Psychologists will tell us that women have a unique sense of body appearance. In a study I did for Playtex, we spent days examining how women feel about their bodies. We did several major think tanks with professionals who study bodies. We even had a sexual healer who worked intimately with partners to help them get through whatever barriers were keeping them from enjoying sex. (This was pre-Viagra.) The group was rounded out with dieticians, trainers, and psychiatrists who specialized in eating disorders. The major conclusion: Whether negative or positive, none of us see ourselves as others see us. This advice is especially important in the case of baby boomers, since we will never see ourselves as old. The implication for marketers: Try to see people as people see themselves and market to that perception.

The Immunity Challenge

Whenever I test a concept that promises to address dust, mites, or any other allergen in the air, in the environment, on clothing, on walls, or in cars, it always gets an overwhelming response. The up-ticks in the numbers of people developing allergies and asthma, big surges in diabetes sufferers, more cancer, and other catastrophic disease survivors should provide major clues about product options in every category. I expect these products will move from the health food stores to the supermarket shelves on aisles boasting nondairy, lactose-free, gluten-free, allergy-free food.

Americans increasingly seek out protection, prevention, or prophylactic benefits from products. Mad cow disease, AIDS, Ebola viruses, peanut allergies, any and all other forms of viral, fungal, bacterial infection and infestation, not to mention cancer in its myriad forms, continue to have us extremely worried. These fears, real and imagined, have wormed their way into our collective psyche. As a result, we're desperately seeking guards against what we perceive as a coming onslaught of pernicious diseases. Foods, beverages, and supplements that promise to boost our immune system or protect us from environmental hazards will become bigger business. In the same way that we're now taking vitamins and dietary supplements to keep from getting ill, we'll be demanding and buying new food products or supplemented ones—cereal with echinacea—that claim to prevent us from contracting diseases.

Where will many of these new foodstuffs come from? Distant rainforests, under the seas, up in mountain tundras—the farther away, the more remote, the greater our faith will be in the product's healing power. But they had better have some natural basis. The consumer today is suspect of chemicals in the environment, foodstuffs, and supplements. We have lived through or been born into a generation where we know well how potent a chemical can be. Good or bad, chemicals can alter moods, re-create natural phenomena, and irreparably change things . . . for the good as well as for the bad.

As we become more educated about food sourcing, ever more particular about what gets tossed into the organic category, we may become more trusting of things that come hermetically sealed in boxes than of foods that are handled throughout the shipping food chain. There will be a big fat yes to heretofore-scorned packaged foods like cheese that can be individually wrapped and protected. More cryovac will appear in display cases. People will say okay to fruits and vegetables that come in nature's own peel-away packaging like bananas and oranges, but goodbye to pears and strawberries unless distributed within a protective wrap that keeps them safe from growth to grocer. More people will regard with suspicion something as seemingly benign as pepper because it's ground on stones that may be infested with a fungus, virus, or bacteria.

The immune-impaired already pay special attention to the source and handling of food, but the fear of contamination is taking root in the general population. I was testing a storyboard that showed a stranger proffering a breath mint to someone in a waiting room situation. Several panelists said that they couldn't even begin to relate to the commercial because they would never accept a breath mint from someone they didn't know.

People whose lives are touched by disease are seizing more control of their treatment, and pharmaceutical companies, buoyed by relaxed regulations, are flexing their newly found marketing and advertising muscle to speak more directly to these consumers. For example, Procrit, a new prescription drug that's advertised as "a natural way to regain red blood cells lost through chemotherapy," obviously believes that there are enough cancer survivors in their viewing audience to pay for a television and a print campaign. With more drug advertising aimed straight at consumers on the horizon, focus groups become more essential in talking meaningfully and sensitively to special groups of consumers.

Redistribution

The hot ideas in marketing will concentrate more on expanded distribution channels for existing products than on baskets of new ones. The future rests in innovative ways and places to get the word out, connect with consumers, and offer convenient methods of procurement. Easy access probably has as much allure for consumers as reasonable pricing. Think beyond the Internet as a venue for products and ponder this news: Consumers are not spending as much time in front of the television screen as you might think. Even though the box is on, very few people sit still to watch. They listen from another room or use TV as background accompaniment to another activity.

Instead, consider when you may have buyers' undivided attention because they're waiting at airports, doctor's offices, or commuter stations. Promote your products in places where consumers conduct the routine of their lives and then try to help potential customers see the link. Spray 'n Wash might market at McDonald's and Pizza Hut—places where stains occur. Woolite might sign a deal to attach packets to plush toys. Ziploc might advertise in travel newsletters. Simply put, sometimes the next big idea is a small connection.

14

FOCUSING IN

A Few Final Thoughts about Focus Groups

Throughout this book, my goal has been to underscore that listening to what your customers have to say and how they say it is crucial to developing and maintaining your brand. Go into focus groups expecting to listen, and I guarantee that you'll learn something new within the first 30 minutes of the dialogue. If you're a sensitive marketer, you'll be able to see the implication between what the consumer tells you and how it can affect your marketing strategies, advertising, and brand development.

Don't go in looking for answers. Go in looking for possibilities and hints and clues about your business. Discount the notion that the consumer will tell you what she needs. Few of us know what we want until we see it. Like the definition of pornography laid out by the judge who said he knew it when he saw it, consumers can tell you when an idea is on the right track, and they can tell you what they've done in the past, but they may not be able to tell you what they want.

Focus groups are useful to diagnose, examine, explore, think about, and directionally understand the probable success of ideas and new thinking. The directional advice is the most important end product of focus groups and can only be achieved by asking "why." It's the "because" that should give the marketer pause . . . or permission.

The consumer will usually prefer what's closest in and most familiar over ideas that are farther out and unfamiliar. Consumers don't like to change any more than marketers. However, if the change respects and coincides with consumer behavior, then the idea is worth pursuit.

I contend that the biggest new convenience product idea of the twentieth century was the Ziploc bag and its zipper-closing cousins. Prior to this, we'd be wrapping, and in the process, tearing and shredding and trying desperately to stop the product that stuck to everything from sticking to itself. Homemakers didn't ask for the bag. They probably wanted a simpler, easier, safer way to keep food fresh, to protect it, and to avoid cutting their hands in the process. The first incarnation, the baggie, was a step in the right direction. It's easier to bag than to wrap, but the new struggle was to keep track of all of those wire twisties. Ziplocs were a vast improvement: They came complete with closure and worked simply and efficiently. However, the self-closing bag didn't find its way to grocery shelves because consumers came up with the idea for — and demanded — such a bag. It landed there and has been a success because someone listened to consumers talk about the mundane, daily battle to wrap up Johnnie's peanut-butter-and-jelly sandwich or save leftover meatloaf.

I love self-closing bags so much I would like to see them in sizes made for postage stamps through mattresses. I would stow my car in one as a preblizzard precaution. I hoard the tiny bags to carry around my vitamins. When I'm traveling to different countries, I use self-closing bags to keep all the currencies straight and then throw in the receipts from each country as well.

Minor modifications on the basic premise have represented added value for the consumer. This incarnation probably came from listening to users talk about the product's benefits and, very importantly, its drawbacks. I also imagine that consumers were asked to think about storage needs when the existing bags might not be used, then asked and probed "Why not?" Those answers are the way the product was refined and extended. So now, we can freeze in them because they're thicker and have a place to write the date; we can stand them up to pour in leftovers; the closure can change color; the closure can be more like a real zipper. (As a pack rat, I found that this incarnation introduced so much value into the bag that I never wanted to throw it out.)

Another great idea—Post-its—was a technical mistake, a process that began as an error and wound up in every home and office around the world because some marketing bright light had listened to how we dog-ear pages, make notes in margins, and get angry if removing tape damages our paper. My point: The consumer does not invent ideas. Focus groups are not the method of choice to hear product ideas from consumers. Even attempts to get at consumer needs are usually a bust. Consumers don't know what they need, or if they do know, you're probably not going to be able to give it to them, because so many needs are wishes. Several rounds of focus groups for General Electric about the perfect washing machine focused on the consumer's views on doing laundry. What the consumer really wanted and needed was a full-time maid. The machine itself was the best part of the process because it *did* the wash. What she really needed was someone to sort it beforehand and fold it and put it away afterward.

Don't look to the consumer to do your work. The marketer continues to show more genius at developing product ideas than the consumer. The consumer is a creature of habit and rarely focuses on the better and the improved, or the new and untried even when asked. On the other hand, the manufacturer often overlooks needs and wishes and desires. Disposable diapers were in development for an entire generation. I doubt that mothers in focus groups expressed a need for disposability. They may have wished for things closer in, because it's hard for consumers to imagine tidal change. The pre-Pampers mothers had baggage that spoke to hard work as part of the mothering process. No pain, no gain meant that mothers had to sacrifice and put up with tons of dirty diapers that needed laundering because it made them feel like a good moms. But as Procter & Gamble listened to groups of women talking about the diaper process, the notion of disposability became clearer and clearer, I'm certain.

Ernest Dichter, the grandfather of focus groups, made a point of telling manufacturers to put on their rational and judgmental hats after leaving a focus group to see if it all made sense. He knew that the way to listen to people in groups was to extract a sense of how they live and how and why they use our products and brands so that we can be more successful marketers and develop more meaningful advertising. Some people love to associate Dichter with the development of the phallic Coke bottle, and even this realization may have come about from careful observation of how panelists handled, or fondled, soft-drink bottles.

Consumers don't give you answers. They provide you with possibilities and insights. Most marketers today, in any room, in any venue, in no matter how many cities worldwide or domestically, listen for opportunities and not for answers. Panelists don't know what they need and what they want anymore than marketers or researchers know.

Panelists are often accused of lying in focus groups. This is so, to the same extent that on occasion we're all guilty of "lying." The old chestnut about the size of the fish we hooked or the enormity of the one that got away attests to this. We all exaggerate, don't we? Well panelists are no different. They exaggerate. They overstate. They speak for show. This is part of our human fiber.

Panelists are us. Although you may not be driven to a confessional, can you really say that there haven't been times when stretching the truth or embroidering on reality didn't come out of your mouth? Take this possibility with you when you're sitting behind the mirror listening to a group of people talk. Imagine how you would act when in a room of strangers, being asked questions that you probably never thought of before, some of which may require you to be vulnerable and express your own sense of self.

So when that woman swears up and down that she wipes her kitchen cabinets every time she finishes cooking, understand why she's exaggerating, and why others in the group are probably nodding in agreement that they do the same thing. Would you be brave enough to admit that you haven't wiped your kitchen cabinets since the blender exploded the last time you were whipping up a Smoothie? I wouldn't.

Psychologists realize that projective techniques encourage people to speak freely because they're not directly talking about themselves. These questioning tools allow consumers to tell the truth without feeling self-conscious and marketers are then able to add dimension and give personality to brands.

So, when we ask panelists to tell how they feel about a brand like French's, first they'll talk about hot dogs and squeeze bottles. Ask them to imagine that French's, the brand, just walked into the room, and then you get the true personality of the brand: It's friendly, American, and childlike and a casual kind of guy. That's the essence of the brand and how advertising agencies get the information to feel good about "Smile, You've Got French's" as a totally appropriate tag line for the brand. You couldn't substitute another brand, either. Does it work if you say, "Smile, You've Got Grey Poupon?" . . . "Smile, You've Got Gulden's?" . . . "Smile, You've Got the Supermarket Brand?" Of course not.

We have to listen carefully to behavior and then we have to put our own sense of things on it to draw a valid conclusion. We may hear inner thoughts in focus groups, and this is better than just measuring behavior and usage, but we have to understand why people are sharing inner thoughts with strangers.

Which brings up the suggestion that the Internet could be an effective way to do focus groups. It certainly presents an opportunity to put people in different parts of the world in the same "room" for a period of time to exchange opinions. Given what I believe about listening beyond the panelists' words, and how strongly I feel about face-to-face market research, it should come as no great surprise to hear that I don't buy into this Internet focus-group premise.

Online focus groups are probably a valuable way to get some quick insight into a topic when your end users are geographically spread out. I can also see its value if you need some quick input from people in special markets who are notoriously busy and un-willing to commit to an out-of-office appointment or to recruit panelists who may wish to maintain a certain degree of anonymity about a lifestyle or behavior (e.g., gays who don't want to come out of the closet or teens who are sexually active).

Generally, though, an in-person interaction remains the best way to understand the human condition and its implications for marketers. To really listen, you have to establish a trust level and allow for spontaneous discussion. The distance between the con-sumer's fingers and his thought process has to get in the way of spontaneity. Trust is an eyeball-to-eyeball thing and too likely to be abused when the participants are anonymous screen names.

The precision of screening for the right panelist will get more finely tuned so that we are assured of speaking to people who not only share similar behaviors and attitudes, but also values and special interests. Generally speaking, recruiting panelists for focus groups is getting more difficult and trickier. Some of it is being done by e-mail as well as by phone, and if this works to find busy people, I have no problem with it.

There will likely continue to be variations on the basic theme of skilled moderators asking consumers for their honest opinions, though the questions might take different formats. Perhaps more projective exercises are on the horizon. More psychological techniques will continue to filter through to focus groups. All of this is good. Moderators are impressionable, and whatever we hear about that may have worked for one moderator, will undoubtedly find its way into other moderators' bag of tricks.

More importantly, focus groups are and should be here to stay, because consumers are here to stay, whether they are sitting in front of a screen, pushing a cart down an aisle, glancing at billboards while in a traffic jam, listening to the radio, watching television, or talking about a new product with their best friend. The focus group is the best way to be there with the consumer. If you're there with your customer and are compassionate with your audience, you get a foot up on your competition because you know more. It will always behoove marketers to try to find out what consumers are doing . . . and why. What they're thinking . . . and why. How they're feeling . . . and why. The best way to do this? Ask them in person. The best way to learn? Listen to everything they say. In fact, go *beyond* listening.

INDEX